THE SPIRITUAL LIVES OF GREAT COMPOSERS

Patrick Kavanaugh

SPARROW

Sparrow Press
Nashville, Tennessee

Library of Congress Cataloging–in–Publication Data

Kavanaugh, Patrick.
    The spiritual lives of great composers / Patrick Kavanaugh.
        p.   cm.
    Includes bibliographical references.
    ISBN 0-917143-08-6 : $12.95
    1. Composer—Religious life. I. Title.
ML390.K23   1991   92-5614
                                        CIP
                                      MN

Published in Nashville, Tennessee, by Sparrow Press,
and distributed in Canada by Christian Marketing Canada, Ltd.

Printed in the United States of America
5   96 95 94

Edited by Beth Spring
Cover Design by Brenda Whitehill
Book Design by Kerry Woo

Table of Contents

Introduction

Music has such spiritual qualities that we should not be surprised at discovering the strong faith many composers possessed. Yet this is a subject which is seldom brought out in the biographies of great musicians or composers. Indeed, one can read about music and study music literature for years without ever being informed of the personal Christian beliefs which many of history's greatest musicians held.

This book, *The Spiritual Lives of Great Composers,* fulfills a tremendous need in the musical world. Its author, Dr. Patrick Kavanaugh, is a notable composer, conductor, lecturer, and Executive Director of the Christian Performing Artists' Fellowship. I have known Patrick for several years, and I am very enthusiastic about his dedication in faith, as well as his personal commitment to excellence. He has spent over five years of research at the Library of Congress in Washington, D.C. to bring together a inspiring chronicle of music's Christian heritage.

There is so much in this book that every musician needs to know. What a joy to find that so many of the great masterpieces we love were written to the glory of God. It strengthens our faith to see the higher purpose that motivated these composers, many of whom faced severe difficulties. Reading about them, we too may sense a mandate to follow the example of those who acknowledged that their talents were a gift from God.

I hope that as you read *The Spiritual Lives of Great Composers* you will be encouraged, as I have been, by the harmony of faith and giftedness that we have in the beauty of music.

Soli Deo Gloria!

- CHRISTOPHER PARKENING

A Word Before

In this book, I have profiled twelve composers who come from a wide variety of backgrounds and beliefs. Yet among them there is a surprising level of agreement on basic Christian beliefs. Even men as dissimilar as Franz Joseph Haydn and Igor Stravinsky appear to hold in common an active spirituality.

This is not to imply that any of these composers lived the exemplary life of a saint. These were real human beings, often coping with very difficult circumstances and with their share of human failings. But each had a sincere faith. The purpose in writing this book is to focus on this often neglected aspect of their lives. Thus, this is a collection of the established, though little known facts concerning the faith of twelve of the influential composers in our history.

Each chapter contains some biographical details in order to provide a background for the beliefs the different composers expressed. The essence of this writing, however, is not about what they *did*, but what they *believed*. There is already an abundance of excellent biographies on each of these composers. (See the Footnotes and Bibliography sections. In the volumes listed, readers can study all the typical details of the composers' careers and music.)

In the twentieth century, so much has been written about the negative side of composers' lives—anecdotes about their conceit, their tempers, their financial troubles and their many failures—that a grossly inaccurate picture is often widely accepted without question. I wish to highlight verifiable aspects of these men's lives as they strove for good, sought to understand God, and found meaningful spiritual purpose in their lives.

Much of the material presented here is not emphasized in typical biographies. Instead, my material has been gathered largely from composers' letters, writings and recollections of these composers' friends and families. Extensive footnotes throughout the material concerning the composers' beliefs have been inserted to assist in further research.

The chapters conclude with some personal thoughts concerning a particularly striking characteristic of each composer's life; a characteristic which may have enabled them to achieve their respective places in history. All too often, studies on distinguished men become mere theoretical exercises, rather than encouraging the enrichment of the reader's (and author's) own progress. Therefore, these sections and the book's conclusion are written with the hope that readers may find inspiration, encouragement and personal application. I have also provided a short section entitled "Recommended Listening," to assist those who may be new to the music of these composers and want to further explore the magnificence of their music.

This book has evolved from a number of experiences with the Christian Performing Artists' Fellowship, with which I serve as the Executive Director. In the spring of 1989, CPAF was asked by the National Portrait Gallery to do a lecture/performance entitled "The Faith of the American Composer." In it, I included the material that appears here concerning Charles Ives and Igor Stravinsky. The following spring, CPAF sponsored several similar lecture/performances at Washington, D.C., universities entitled "The Spiritual Lives of Great Composers." For these events, I added the material on Bach, Mozart, Beethoven, and Wagner. The chapters on Handel, Haydn, Schubert, Mendelssohn, Liszt, and Dvorak were later researched for the program notes of certain CPAF performances.

Of course there are many more great masters than this book contains. The extensive research that goes into these articles will continue as part of the ongoing work of CPAF.

I hope this book will shed light on an important, but so often overlooked subject of music history: the spiritual beliefs that underscore these composers' contributions to Western culture.

- PATRICK KAVANAUGH

January, 1992

To my dear wife and best friend, Barbara.

"It pleased the Almighty, to whose great Holy Will I submit myself with Christian submission."

1

GEORGE FRIDERIC
HANDEL

1685 - 1759

In a small London house on Brook Street, a servant sighs with resignation as he arranges a tray full of food he assumes will not be eaten. For more than a week, he has faithfully continued to wait on his employer, an eccentric composer, who spends hour after hour isolated in his own room. Morning, noon, and evening the servant delivers appealing meals to the composer, and returns later to find the bowls and platters largely untouched.

Once again, he steels himself to go through the same routine, muttering under his breath about how oddly temperamental musicians can be. As he swings open the door to the composer's room, the servant stops in his tracks.

The startled composer, tears streaming down his face, turns to his servant and cries out, "I did think I did see all Heaven before me, and the great God Himself." George Frideric Handel had just finished writing a movement which would take its place in history as the "Hallelujah Chorus."

If Handel's father had had his way, the "Hallelujah Chorus" would never have been written. His father was a "surgeon-barber" — a no-nonsense, practical man who was determined to send his son to law school. Even though young Handel showed extraordinary musical talent as a child, his father refused for several years to permit him to take lessons.

George Frideric was born in 1685, a contemporary of Bach, a fellow German, and was raised a fellow Lutheran, yet they were never to meet. Though numerous books on the lives of great composers begin with Bach, in fact, Handel was born several weeks earlier, on February 23, 1685.

When the boy was eight or nine years old, a duke heard him play an organ postlude following a worship service. Handel's father was summarily requested to provide formal music training for the boy. By the time Handel turned 12, he had written his first composition and was so proficient at the organ that he substituted, on occasion, for his own teacher.

Young Handel continued to master the clavichord, oboe, and violin, as well as composition through the years. In 1702 he entered the University of Halle to study law out of respect for his late father's desire. But he soon abandoned his legal studies and devoted himself entirely to music.

He became a violinist and composer in a Hamburg opera theater, then traveled to Italy from 1706 to 1710 under the patronage of their music-loving courts. In Rome, he wrote "The Resurrection," an oratorio in which religious themes emerged for the first time in Handel's music. While in Italy, Handel met some of the eminent musicians of his day, notably Domenico Scarlatti.

In 1712, after a short stay at the court of Hanover, he moved to England, where he lived for the rest of his life. There he anglicized his name from its original spelling, Georg Friedrich. He dropped the *diaeresis* originally on the "a" of his surname, and this led to various spellings by different publishers: Haendel, Hendel and so on.

Handel was the sort of individual who stands out in a crowd. Large-boned and loud, he often wore an enormous white wig with curls cascading to his shoulders. When he spoke, his English was replete with colorful snatches of German, French and Italian.

Although Handel wrote his greatest music in England, he suffered personal setbacks there as well. Falling in and out of favor with changing monarchs, competing with established English composers, and dealing with fickle, hard-to-please audiences left him confronting bankruptcy more than once.

Yet Handel retained his sense of humor through virtually any hardship. Once, just as an oratorio of his was about to begin, several of his friends gathered to console him about the extremely sparse audience attracted to the performance. "Never mind," Handel joked to his friends. "The music will sound the better" due to the improved acoustics of a very empty concert hall!

Like his fellow composer Bach, Handel was also renowned as a virtuoso organist. One Sunday, after attending worship services at a country church,

Handel asked the organist's permission to play a postlude. As the congregation was leaving the church, Handel began to play with such expertise that the people reclaimed their seats and refused to withdraw. The regular organist finally stopped him, saying that Handel had better not play the postlude after all, if the people were ever to get home.

Audiences for Handel's compositions were unpredictable, and even the Church of England attacked him for what they considered his notorious practice of writing biblical dramas such as *Esther* and *Israel in Egypt* to be performed in secular theaters. His occasional commercial successes soon met with financial disaster, as rival opera companies competed for the ticket holders of London. He drove himself relentlessly to recover from one failure after another, and finally his health began to fail. By 1741 he was swimming in debt. It seemed certain he would land in debtor's prison.

On April 8 of that year, he gave what he considered his farewell concert. Miserably discouraged, he felt forced to retire from public activities at the age of 56. Then two unforeseen events converged to change his life. A wealthy friend, Charles Jennings, gave Handel a libretto based on the life of Christ, taken entirely from the Bible.[1] He also received a commission from a Dublin charity to compose a work for a benefit performance.

Handel set to work composing on August 22 in his little house on Brook Street in London.[2] He grew so absorbed in the work that he rarely left his room, hardly stopping to eat. Within six days Part One was complete. In nine days more he had finished Part Two, and in another six, Part Three. The orchestration was completed in another two days.[3] In all, 260 pages of manuscript were filled in the remarkably short time of 24 days.

Sir Newman Flower, one of Handel's many biographers, summed up the consensus of history: "Considering the immensity of the work, and the short time involved, it will remain, perhaps forever, the greatest feat in the whole history of music composition."[4] Handel's title for the commissioned work was, simply, *Messiah*.

Handel never left his house for those three weeks.[5] A friend who visited him as he composed found him sobbing with intense emotion.[6] Later, as Handel groped for words to describe what he had experienced, he quoted St. Paul, saying, "Whether I was in the body or out of my body when I wrote it I know not."[7]

Messiah premiered on April 13, 1742, as a charitable benefit, raising 400 pounds and freeing 142 men from debtor's prison.[8] A year later, Handel staged it in London. Controversy emanating from the Church of England continued to plague Handel,[9] yet the King of England attended the performance. As the first notes of the triumphant "Hallelujah Chorus" rang out, the king rose. Following royal protocol, the entire audience stood too, initiating a tradition which has lasted for more than two centuries.

Soon after this, Handel's fortunes began to increase dramatically, and his hard-won popularity remained constant until his death. By the end of his long life, *Messiah* was firmly established in the standard repertoire. Its influence on other composers would be extraordinary. When Haydn later heard the "Hallelujah Chorus", he wept like a child, and exclaimed, "He is the master of us all!"

Handel personally conducted more than thirty performances of *Messiah*. Many of these concerts were benefits for the Foundling Hospital, of which Handel was a major benefactor.[10] The thousands of pounds Handel's performances of *Messiah* raised for charity led one biographer to note: "*Messiah* has fed the hungry, clothed the naked, fostered the orphan...more than any other single musical production in this or any country."[11] Another wrote, "Perhaps the works of no other composer have so largely contributed to the relief of human suffering."[12]

This work has had an uncanny spiritual impact on the lives of its listeners. One writer has stated that *Messiah's* music and message "has probably done more to convince thousands of mankind that there is a God about us than all the theological works ever written."[13]

The composer's own assessment, more than any other, may best capture his personal aspirations for his well-loved work. Following the first London performance of *Messiah*, Lord Kinnoul congratulated Handel on the excellent "entertainment." Handel replied, "My Lord, I should be sorry if I only entertain them. I wish to make them better."[14]

The religious beliefs of the composer who created the world's most popular religious masterpiece have puzzled many musicologists. In an era when Christian musicians typically worked for local churches, this composer of secular opera, chamber, and orchestral music did not fit the usual pattern. Yet he was a devout follower of Christ and widely known for his concern for others.[15] Handel's morals were above reproach.[16] At church he was often seen "on his knees, expressing by his looks and gesticulations the utmost fervor of devotion."[17]

Yet the very persistence that kept Handel going through the worst of times made him obstinate and temperamental when he encountered opposition. A confirmed bachelor, Handel was reputed to swear in several languages when moved to wrath (usually by singers). At the same time, he was equally quick to admit his own fault and apologize.

Handel was known for his modest and straightforward opinion of himself and his talent. When a friend unwittingly commented on the dreariness of some music he had heard at the Vauxhall Gardens, Handel rejoined, "You are right, sir, it is pretty poor stuff. I thought so myself when I wrote it."

His friend Sir John Hawkins recorded that Handel "throughout his life manifested a deep sense of religion. In conversation he would frequently declare the pleasure he felt in setting the Scriptures to music, and how contemplating the many sublime passages in the Psalms had contributed to his edification."[18] In one of his few surviving letters, Handel comforts his brother-in-law on the death of Handel's mother: "It pleased the Almighty, to whose great Holy Will I submit myself with Christian submission."[19]

Known universally for his generosity and concern for those who suffered, Handel donated freely to charities even in times when he faced personal financial ruin. He was a relentless optimist whose faith in God sustained him through every difficulty. Raised a sincere Lutheran, he harbored no sectarian animosities and steered clear of denominational disagreements.[20] Once, defending himself before a quarrelsome archbishop, Handel simply replied "I have read my Bible very well, and will choose for myself."[21]

A few days before Handel died, he expressed his desire to die on Good Friday, "in the hopes of meeting his good God, his sweet Lord and Savior, on the day of his Resurrection."[22] He lived until the morning of Good Saturday, April 14, 1759. His death came only eight days after his final performance, at which he had conducted his masterpiece, *Messiah.*

His close friend James Smyth wrote, "He died as he lived—a good Christian, with a true sense of his duty to God and to man, and in perfect charity with all the world."[23] Handel was buried in Westminster Abbey, with over 3,000 in attendance at his funeral.[24] A statue erected there shows him holding the manuscript for the solo that opens Part Three of *Messiah,* "I know that my Redeemer liveth."[25]

SOME THOUGHTS ON HANDEL: RESILIENCE

When reviewing the lives of great figures in history, it is tempting to focus only on the end results of their lives, glossing over the periods between the masterpieces they produced. Because "the end of the story" is a matter of record, it may be difficult to appreciate the struggles that threatened to make the story far shorter. In Handel's case especially, had he not possessed an amazing ability to bounce back from repeated disaster, such well-loved works as *Messiah* and the *Royal Fireworks Music* would have never been written.

How often Handel must have felt like giving up! What fits of depression his many failures would have caused an average composer. To a man who knew he had but one great talent, seeing that talent go unrewarded so often must have been profoundly perplexing. And to see other London composers, whom he knew to have less genius, enjoying the success that eluded him for so many years—must have driven Handel to extreme exasperation. Yet through all the frustrating years before his final successes, Handel simply refused to quit.

And—as if blows inflicted by his competitors were not painful enough—Handel suffered from an onslaught of attacks within his own camp. For a devoted Christian to have come under censure by the principle church of his time must have been bitterly distressing. Even after *Messiah* was becoming well-known, as great a religious figure as John Newton (composer of the hymn "Amazing Grace"), preached every Sunday for over a year against the "secular" performances of this biblical oratorio. Yet Handel did not respond by counter-attacking his Anglican brothers. Though he remained a Lutheran, he "would often speak of it as one of the great felicities of his life that he was settled in a country where no man suffers any molestation or inconvenience on account of his religious principles."

Handel refused to be deterred by setbacks, attacks, illnesses, or even severe financial woes. It is a tribute to the faith and optimism Handel possessed, relying on God as he worked to overcome significant obstacles and to create music which is universally cherished today.

RECOMMENDED LISTENING:

Orchestral Music: 12 concerti grossi; Water Music; Royal Fireworks Music.

Chamber Music: 6 Sonatas for Recorder; 8 Sonatas for Violin.

Keyboard: Suite in D minor; Chaconne in G.

Oratorio: Messiah; Israel in Egypt; Judas Maccabaeus; Esther.

"*Where there is devotional music, God is always at hand with His gracious presence.*"

2

JOHANN SEBASTIAN
BACH

1685 - 1750

Through the autumn countryside of Germany, a young man of twenty walks briskly, soaking up the faded October sun and crunching fallen leaves underfoot. It is 1705, and the young man is on his way from Arnstadt to Lubeck—a 200 mile trek. The miles pass quickly as he anticipates the music he is determined to hear. One of the great organists of his day, Dietrich Buxtehude, will be performing evening musical devotions at the Cathedral this time of year, in preparation for Advent.

Traveling on foot to hear concerts was nothing new to this young organist; many times he had tramped thirty miles to Hamburg to hear the renowned organist Reincken, and had even walked sixty miles to Celle to attend programs of French music. But to hear Buxtehude! For this opportunity, he needed at least a month's leave of absence from his position as a church organist. His superiors had grudgingly consented, after the organist entreated them relentlessly for the necessary leave.

Arriving at Lubeck, footsore yet charged with excitement, the young musician drinks in the organ concerts of the master with a profound sense of personal inspiration. He sends word back to his employer at Arnstadt that he needs two months off instead of just one, knowing he risks being fired.

> Three years after this experience, he announces his ulti-
> mate purpose in life: to create "well-regulated church music to
> the glory of God." With an insatiable appetite to learn and a
> propensity for ceaseless work, he set about doing just that. His
> name was Johann Sebastian Bach.

Throughout history, Bach has been acclaimed as *the* Christian composer, almost a kind of "patron saint" for church musicians. All around the world, he is recognized as one of the greatest composers who has ever lived. This is not to say there were no great spiritual composers before Bach; he actually represents the culmination of centuries abounding with Christian music.

The sheer number of works he composed is staggering, however, and so is their diversity. They include chorales, cantatas, masses, oratorios, passions, concerti, and solo works for virtually every instrument of his day. Bach was prolific in other areas of life as well: he worked in a variety of demanding jobs (often with many extra-musical duties), and fathered twenty children, several of whom also matured into noted musicians.

When Johann Sebastian was born in 1685 in Eisenach, Germany, the Bach name was already synonymous with the musical trade. More than fifty musicians bearing that name are remembered by musicologists today. Even as a boy, Bach appeared eager to find expression for his emerging musical talent.

Orphaned at the age of nine, Johann moved in with an older brother, and his musical training began. He soon developed into an outstanding singer, and demonstrated a remarkable ability to play the organ, the violin and numerous other instruments. Bach's brother owned a set of compositions which he forbid the younger Bach to use. Perhaps because it was placed off limits, that musical manuscript grew irresistibly attractive to the young musician.

And so for weeks, Bach stole the precious pages and hid them in his room, where he stayed up late night after night copying the musical scores by moonlight. When his brother discovered the copied pages, he angrily confiscated them. But Bach had already gleaned valuable lessons in composition, as well as discipline and devotion to music, from the clandestine exercise.

Throughout his life he was known much more as an organist than a composer. Amazing to us, only ten of Bach's original compositions were published during his lifetime. It was not until the nineteenth century that his brilliance as a composer was truly appreciated. Only then would he be revered by such masters as Beethoven, who claimed, "His name ought not to be Bach

("Bach" is the German word for "brook"), but *ocean*, because of his infinite and inexhaustible wealth of combinations and harmonies."

Like so many other masters throughout history, Bach's personality had many facets. On one hand, he was free from personal vanity, was generous and encouraging toward his many pupils. The Bach family also had a great reputation for their hospitality. His first biographer, Forkel, notes, "These sociable virtues, together with his great artistic fame, caused his house to be rarely free from visitors."[1]

Once, when an acquaintance praised Bach's wonderful skill as an organist, he replied with characteristic humility and wit: "There is nothing very wonderful about it. You have only to hit the right notes at the right moment and the instrument does the rest."[2]

Yet he could be stubborn and irritable, especially with an unappreciative employer or an incompetent musician. At the age of twenty, Bach ridiculed a colleague by calling him "Kippelfagottist" — a "nanny-goat bassoonist". The offended musician picked up a stick and struck Bach, who drew his sword. A full-blown duel would have ensued, but fortunately, friends who saw the argument intensify threw themselves between the two adversaries to keep them apart.

Bach spent his entire life in Germany, working primarily as a church musician. For the two centuries prior, this region had been permeated by the legacy of Martin Luther, with his radical emphasis on a living, personal, Bible-based Christianity. Luther himself had been a musician, declaring music to be second only to the gospel itself. Bach was to be the Reformer's greatest musical disciple.

Bach resoundingly echoed the convictions of Luther, claiming that "Music's only purpose should be for the glory of God and the recreation of the human spirit."[3] As he set about composing, he would frequently initial his blank manuscript pages with the marking, "J.J." (*Jesu Juva* — "Help me, Jesus"),[4] or "I.N.J." (*In Nomine Jesu* — "In the name of Jesus").[5] At the manuscript's end, Bach routinely initialed the letters "S.D.G." (*Soli Deo Gloria* — "To God alone, the glory").[6] To Bach, these were not trite religious slogans, but sincere expressions of personal devotion.

It is clear that Bach possessed a deep, personal religious faith.[7] Indeed, it appears his entire life revolved around his spiritual convictions.[8] As one biographer has stated, "The focus of his emotional life was undoubtedly in religion, and in the service of religion through music."[9]

Bach's surviving letters also contain many references to his devout faith.[10]

The love he felt for his large family is evident in a heart-rending letter Bach wrote on behalf of an erring son who had incurred large debts and then left his town: "What can I do or say more, my warnings having failed, and my loving care and help having proved unavailing? I can only bear my cross in patience and commend my undutiful boy to God's mercy, never doubting that He will hear my sorrow-stricken prayer and in His good time bring my son to understand that the path of conversion leads to Him."[11]

His famous composer son, Carl Philipp Emanuel Bach, once claimed that the entire Bach family "were in the habit of beginning all things with religion".[12] Nothing in life, however mundane, was considered to be unspiritual. This is shown in a humorous poem Bach penned about his tobacco smoking, which ends:

> "On land, on sea, at home, abroad,
> I smoke my pipe and worship God."[13]

In his spiritual outlook, Bach made no real distinction between sacred and secular music. For instance, at the beginning of such a "secular" work as his *Little Organ Book*, he wrote this dedication: "To God alone the praise be given for what's herein to man's use written."[14] His *Little Clavier Book*, like so many of his compositions, was inscribed "In the Name of Jesus".[15]   Often, his compositions would contain chiastic structures, such as A B C D E D C B A. The visual equivalent of the resulting musical form appears as a cross.[16]

Bach was a master of "word-painting", and used a large repertoire of musical devices to enhance the meaning of the text he was setting to music. Of the hundreds of examples of this technique, perhaps the best known is from his *St. Matthew Passion*. In this sublime work, Bach invokes a "divine halo" impression around the figure of Christ by having the strings play long, quiet tones whenever the lines of Jesus are sung. This continues without exception until Jesus' line from the cross, "My God, my God, why have you forsaken me?" At this crucial moment, when Christ's humanity is supreme, the halo of strings is removed, and the emotional effect is unforgettable.

Another memorable scene is found in his colossal *Mass in B Minor*. Toward the end of the dramatic "Crucifixus" movement, the voices and instruments quietly sink into their lowest registers as the body of Jesus is musically lowered into the tomb. This is immediately followed by an explosion of blazing glory in the "Et Resurrexit", an effect composers have copied for centuries.

Even humor was skillfully used when Bach set the Scriptures to music. In his *Magnificat*, as Bach was setting the Latin words of "He has filled the hungry with good things, but the rich he has sent away empty", he had a clever idea. To depict the word *inanes* (empty), he has the flutes abruptly stop playing and leaves but one note in the continuo to fill up the emptiness of the last bar of music! Surely he could not resist a smile as he added this touch to his masterpiece.

As a sincere Lutheran, Bach was a devoted reader of the Bible and other religious volumes. His personal library contained 83 books, inventoried at his death. All of them explored spiritual matters; besides the Bible, there were two different editions of Martin Luther's collected works and dozens of books by Luther's disciples and champions of the seventeenth and eighteenth centuries.[17]

Bach sought spiritual connections between his faith and his art. Even in the midst of study, his pen was rarely still. He inserted a marginal note in his biblical commentary on 1 Chronicles 25, in which King David sets apart musicians for the temple worship: "This chapter is the true foundation for all God-pleasing music."[18] At the conclusion of 1 Chronicles, he noted, "Splendid proof that...music was instituted by the Spirit of God through David."[19]

Another of the composer's favorite passages must have been 2 Chronicles 5:13, describing a temple worship service in ancient Israel with these words: "The trumpeters and singers joined in unison, as with one voice, to give praise and thanks to the Lord. ... Then the temple of the Lord was filled with a cloud, and the priests could not perform their service...for the glory of the Lord filled the temple of God." As Bach paused to contemplate this scripture, he wrote in the margin of his commentary, "Where there is devotional music, God is always at hand with his gracious presence."[20]

A religious controversy in Bach's day was touched off by a movement known as Pietism. The fervency of this anti-ritual group appealed to Bach, who held other doctrines in common with it, including a deep mysticism[21], and an almost passionate longing for death.[22] But the Pietists were incorrigible "art-haters," calling the church cantata a "sinful abomination."[23] Bach could never align himself with a movement which he considered at odds with the biblical view of music.

Bach was from first to last a church musician. At the height of his fame, he left the only secular position he ever held, as *Capellmeister* of the court of Prince Leopold. He chose instead an obscure position as Cantor at a church in Leipzig, where he would again be cloistered in his unacclaimed but beloved world of church music.

Bach's eyes began failing toward the end of his life, and by age 65 he was completely blind. He died in relative obscurity in 1750, and his grave was not even marked.[24] His last work, dictated from his bed, was a chorale entitled "Before Thy Throne I Come."[25]

SOME THOUGHTS ON BACH: PRODUCTIVITY

Bach's musical genius stands as a marvel through more than two centuries since his death. Yet the musician did not believe that he was singled out for unsurpassed genius. He told a student, "Just practice diligently, and it will go very well. You have five fingers on each hand just as healthy as mine."

When asked the secret of his genius, he answered simply, "I was made to work; if you are equally industrious you will be equally successful." It is doubtful whether anyone in the world of music has matched Bach's industriousness. When his multitudinous scores were finally collected and published, the job took the *Bach Gesellschaft* 46 years, and the completed edition filled 60 huge volumes.

Yet all of his composing took place while Bach was fulfilling dozens of other tasks: working as an organist, a conductor, a music director, a private instructor, even a teacher of Latin to young boys—not to mention raising a large family and moving from post to post. The inspiration and beauty of his music are abundantly apparent, yet the real mystery of Bach's life as a composer concerns *how* he found the actual time to write it all, and still more to have created so many masterpieces cherished through the ages.

Bach personified the German Protestant work ethic. *I was made to work* could have been his life motto. Yet he was never known to speak a word of complaint; on the contrary, he seems to have reveled in his decades of musical toil, dating from the time he copied forbidden compositions at night. And even in his final year of life, after an operation left him sightless, Bach worked frantically to revise his great choral fantasies.

Bach's devotion to God and his drive to express that devotion musically gave the world a gift for all to appreciate. His productivity forged a musical legacy which Richard Wagner would someday appraise as "the most stupendous miracle in all music."

RECOMMENDED LISTENING:

Orchestral Music: 6 Brandenburg concertos; 4 suites.

Keyboard music: The Well-Tempered Clavier; Goldberg Variations; 6 French suites; 6 English suites; 6 partitas.

Organ Music: Toccata and Fugue in D minor.

Choral Music: The Passion According to St. Matthew; Mass in B minor; Magnificat; Christmas Oratorio; Easter Oratorio; Church cantatas, notably No. 4 ("Christ lag in Todesbanden"), No. 80 ("Ein' feste Burg ist unser Gott"), and No. 140 ("Wachet Auf").

"Since God
has given me
a cheerful heart,
He will
forgive me
for serving
Him cheerfully."

3

FRANZ JOSEPH
HAYDN

1732 - 1809

The Prince is enjoying himself immensely. He spent eleven million *florins* to build his magnificent castle and estate in the countryside near Vienna, and he indulged his new home with every conceivable luxury. And now, relaxed and surrounded by his treasures, Prince Paul Esterhazy listens to his private orchestra perform a new symphony.

He gazes at the musicians he retains year-round and congratulates himself on having recently put them in their place. *How dare they complain*, the Prince muses, *and ask for more time off to visit their families? After all, I treat them just like family right here....*

The Prince's reverie is broken all at once when two of the musicians stop playing, snuff out the candles on their music stands, and walk off the stage. *Wait! What is going on here?* the Prince breathes aloud. As he watches, two more musicians, and then two more make their exits as well. The Prince jumps to his feet, perplexed, and turns his attention to the conductor, who seems singularly unruffled by these abrupt departures.

Prince Esterhazy slowly takes his seat again as the light of understanding dawns. *What had the conductor called this new symphony he composed?* the Prince wondered. *Oh yes, the "Farewell."* Finally, only two violins are left, and the conductor himself begins gathering up his score and preparing to leave.

By now the Prince has taken the hint. Before his conductor leaves the room, the Prince stops him. He now gives his approval to the musicians' demand for extra leave time. The Prince's music director and conductor, Franz Joseph Haydn, had made his point.

Haydn, one of the most successful and famous composers in history, came from the most humble surroundings. He was born in the small town of Rohrau, in lower Austria, to parents who loved music but were quite poor. They recognized Haydn's musical talent when he was very young, and at age six he was sent to a nearby town for musical training. Two years later he became a choir boy in Vienna, and for the next nine years he sang in the famed St. Stephen's Cathedral in Vienna.

When his voice began changing in 1749, his secure life as a choir boy ended. He was dismissed from the cathedral and soon found himself, at age 17, miserable and penniless. Haydn lived hand to mouth by giving lessons and playing the violin for Vienna serenades.

Haydn had been raised a Roman Catholic, and later in life he frequently expressed gratitude to his parents for "bringing him up in the fear of God."[1] His parents urged Haydn to become a priest,[2] and at one point he agreed to enter the Servite order.[3] But he concluded that God's call on his life did not require him to enter the priesthood; instead, it meant training and exercising his prodigious musical talents. One day he wrote, "I know that God has favored me, and recognize it thankfully. I also believe that I have done my duty and have been of use to the world through my works. Let others do the same!"[4]

In the eighteenth century, there were few concert halls and public performances in Vienna. The best way for a musician to make a living outside the church was to be hired by a rich nobleman. It took time, but Haydn finally made contact with important musicians of his day. His first regular job was as music director for the court of Count Morzin.

Then in 1761, the turning point in Haydn's life came when he was hired by Prince Paul Esterhazy. Moving to the Prince's grand country estate marked the beginning of nearly three decades during which Haydn would spend his musical life in the finest circumstances a composer could desire.

While he was employed by the Esterhazy nobility, Haydn produced an enormous amount of music. He would complete 104 symphonies, 76 string quartets, masses, oratorio, opera, concerti, and dozens of chamber works. It is no wonder he has become known among music historians as the "Father of the Symphony," the "Father of the String Quartet," and even the "Father of the Sonata."

For Haydn, music brought unparalleled purpose and joy to life. In contrast, his home life was a source of pain and unfulfilled promise. As a young man, he fell in love with a girl—who later stunned him by entering a convent. Impulsively, he proposed to her older sister, and she agreed to marry him. The two newlyweds proved utterly incompatible. Haydn's new bride had so little regard for his composing genius that she cut up his manuscripts to use for hair-curling papers!

Eventually they agreed to a separation. Nonetheless, Haydn remained faithful, never considering divorce. He generously supported his wife throughout his life and in his will. He is remembered never to have spoken an unkind word about her.

Haydn's disappointing attempt at marriage did not deter his zest for composing or hinder his deep faith in God. In many ways, his work and his faith were intricately linked. In the morning, Haydn awakened early and prayed on his knees daily, before beginning to compose.[5]

Seated at his clavier, Haydn searched for an idea—a theme, an image to set to music. "If it soon comes without much difficulty, it expands," Haydn once said. "But if it does not make progress I try to find out if I have erred in some way or other, thereby forfeiting grace; and I pray for mercy until I feel that I am forgiven."[6]

In recalling his struggles while composing a certain sacred work, Haydn wrote, "I prayed to God—not like a miserable sinner in despair—but calmly, slowly. In this I felt that an infinite God would surely have mercy on his finite creature, pardoning dust for being dust. These thoughts cheered me up. I experienced a sure joy so confident that as I wished to express the words of the prayer, I could not express my joy, but gave vent to my happy spirits and wrote above the *Miserere*, 'Allegro.'"[7]

His music is so ebullient in temperament that it was actually criticized by more puritanical members of the church. Haydn's reply was characteristic: "Since God has given me a cheerful heart, He will forgive me for serving him cheerfully."[8]

When Haydn pondered the reality of a God who cared for him, and for all people, he said his heart "leapt for joy."[9] He could not prevent his music from expressing the same exuberance—even when the music was conveying one of Christianity's more somber themes.

Once, as he was setting to music the familiar words from the Mass: *Agnus Dei, qui tollis peccata mundi* ("Lamb of God, who takes away the sins of the world"), Haydn said he was seized by an "uncontrollable gladness."[10] He even had to apologize to Empress Marie Therese on this point, explaining that the certainty of God's grace had made him so happy that he wrote a joyful melody to accompany the sober words.[11]

It was always his goal, he said, to "depict Divinity through love and goodness."[12] One of Haydn's many sacred works, the *Stabat Mater*, was among his favorites because it had been composed to fulfill a religious vow made after recovering from a serious illness.[13]

Like Bach before him, Haydn began most of his scores with the words, *In Nomini Jesu*,[14] and ended them with *Laus Deo* or *Soli Deo Gloria*.[15] His close friend, Georg August Griesinger, said that Haydn was "loyally devoted to the faith in which he was raised. He was strongly convinced in his heart that all human destiny was under God's guiding hand, that God rewards the good and the evil, and that all talents come from above."[16]

Haydn's unique combination of faith and work may have achieved its culmination with his oratorio, *The Creation*, finished at the age of 66. *The Creation* was written to inspire "the adoration and worship of the Creator," Haydn wrote, and to put the listener "in a frame of mind where he is most susceptible to the kindness and omnipotence of the Creator."[17]

Haydn later recalled, "Never was I so devout as when I composed *The Creation*. I knelt down each day to pray to God to give me strength for my work."[18] He told a friend, "When I was working on *The Creation* I felt so impregnated with the Divine certainty, that before sitting down to the piano, I would quietly and confidently pray to God to grant me the talent that was needed to praise him worthily."[19]

Haydn was a faithful Catholic, yet his life and his music were non-sectarian. A Protestant clergyman who knew him wrote that Haydn "appeared to me to be a religious character, and not only attentive to the forms and usages of his church, but under the influence of a devotional spirit." This man, the Reverend C. J. Latrobe, considered Haydn "his spiritual father."[20] Though the composer knew the Mass by heart,[21] at least once he even changed Catholic texts to place a greater emphasis on Christ.[22]

At the urging of his devoted friend, Mozart, Haydn once joined the Order of Freemasons in Vienna.[23] His interest in this group waned quickly, and he never attended any of their secret meetings.[24] His life and music were for all the world. He told a group of musicians who banded together to play his *Creation*,

"There are so few happy and contented people here below, sorrow and anxiety pursue them from everywhere; perhaps your work may, some day, become a spring from which the careworn may draw a few moment's rest and refreshment."[25]

Haydn always insisted that his talents were an unmerited gift from God. "Our Almighty Father had endowed me with so much faculty in music that even in my sixth year I stood up like a man and sang Masses in the church choir," he once reminisced.[26] In an autobiographical sketch, he concluded, "I offer all my praises to Almighty God, for I owe them to Him alone; my sole wish is to neither offend my neighbor, nor my gracious Prince, nor above all our merciful God."[27]

Toward the end of his productive life, Haydn's faith increased in fervor. He approached death calmly, telling his friend Griesinger, "I only have to wait like a child for the time when God calls me to Himself."[28] As an old man, he gave the following advice to the Vienna choirboys, "Be good and industrious and serve God continually."[29]

He also kept his humor to the end. In 1805, a rumor spread that Haydn had died. Many composers wrote memorial pieces, and in Paris a special concert was arranged, including Mozart's *Requiem*. When Haydn found out about his widely rumored death, he sent a letter thanking the musicians for their well-meant gestures. He added, "Had I only known of it in time, I could have traveled to Paris to conduct the *Requiem* myself!"

Joseph Haydn died peacefully in 1809, soon after Napoleon occupied Vienna. Showing deep regard for the composer's universal celebrity, this conquering enemy of Austria placed an honor guard at Haydn's home and assigned his highest officers to Haydn's funeral. His will—which generously remembered people whom he had not seen for decades—began, "In the Name of the Most Holy Trinity," and continued, "My soul I bequeath to its all-bountiful Creator."[30]

The last performance Haydn attended was *The Creation*, on March 27, 1808. As the music ended and the audience applauded enthusiastically, Haydn lifted his hands toward heaven and said, "Not from me—from there, above, comes everything."[31]

SOME THOUGHTS ON HAYDN: HUMILITY

By the time Haydn died, he had become recognized as the greatest living composer. From the most insignificant of beginnings he achieved universal acclaim, and from a childhood of poverty he worked his way into considerable wealth. Yet throughout his long climb, he remained the same modest and reserved man who had played for his supper on the streets of Vienna.

Once, late in life, when Haydn met a devotee who heaped praise upon him, Haydn cut him off. "Do not speak so to me. You see only a man whom God has granted talent and a good heart." Never ashamed of his humble up-bringing, he would often go to church in his shirt sleeves, like a peasant. In the class conscious society in which he spent his entire adult life, how refreshing it must have been to be with a self-made genius whose ego did not grow with his fortune.

Perhaps the secret to Haydn's humility lay in the unassuming contentment he displayed in all circumstances. Long before his later prosperity, he told a friend, "When I sit at my old worm eaten piano, I envy no king in his happiness." The simplicity of this great genius was sincere. When he grew old, he said, "I have associated with kings, emperors, and many great gentlemen and have heard many flattering things from them; but I do not wish to live on an intimate footing with such persons, and I prefer people of my own status."

Haydn simply refused to be lured by the trappings of the world. He was content with what he had, and he made a habit of expressing thanks to God and to those around him. Without complaint, he remained accessible to the musicians who worked under him and often presented their needs to their common employer. Even when the King of England George III complimented Haydn on the great deal of music he had created, the reply was simply, "Yes, Sire, a great deal more than is good." Long after his fame was established, Haydn all but disdained his wages, given by the Prince to his "undeserving self." In Haydn's case, this was not a mere expression of servility, but an outgrowth of his true attitude of mind.

Without this humility, his climb to success and wealth might have resulted in much less music for posterity to enjoy. He could have rested on past laurels, retired early, and enjoyed the good life. Instead, he chose to work almost to the very end of his life, living unpretentiously and giving generously to others. Haydn composed some of his finest masterpieces in his sixties and seventies, including *The Creation*, *The Seasons*, and *The Seven Last Words of Christ*.

RECOMMENDED LISTENING:

Orchestral Music: 104 Symphonies, notably No. 45 ("Farewell"), and No. 94 ("Surprise").

Chamber Music: 83 String Quartets, notably Op. 76, #3 ("The Emperor"), and Op. 76, #4 ("Sunrise").

Piano Music: 52 Piano Sonatas, notably No. 49 ("Genzinger").

Oratorio: The Creation, The Seasons.

"God is ever before my eyes. I realize His omnipotence and I fear His anger; but I also recognize His love, His compassion, and His tenderness towards His creatures."

4

WOLFGANG AMADEUS MOZART

1756 - 1791

The Papal Choir excelled during its Holy Week performances, leaving the worshippers breathless in reverent praise. In one pew, a young boy visiting the Vatican leans forward expectantly, transported by the music.

He listens intently as the choir sings its annual presentation of a beloved *Miserere*, a composition protected by papal decree. By law, this work could not be performed elsewhere, and the only manuscript of the music was closely guarded by the Vatican. Anyone who attempted to copy it would be punished immediately by excommunication.

After the performance, the young Austrian lad settles down at a desk in his room and writes out—from memory—every note of the elaborate *Miserere* he had just heard. News of this facsimile makes its way back to the Pope, and the Vatican buzzes with speculation over what would happen next.

The boy's punishment? Instead of excommunicating the boy for his feat of phenomenal genius, the Pope presents young Wolfgang Amadeus Mozart with a select Vatican honor: the coveted Cross of the Order of the Golden Spur.

The very term "child prodigy" seems to bear a special affinity for Johann Chrysostom Wolfgang Amadeus Mozart, born in Salzburg, Austria, in 1756.

At age three he amused himself at the keyboard. At four his formal training began, and within a year he was improvising minuets. When he turned six his loving but ambitious father arranged the first of many concert tours in which little Wolfgang performed for the delighted courts and nobility of Europe.

An advertisement for one of Mozart's child performances drew crowds of curious bystanders: "He will play a concerto on the violin, and will accompany symphonies on the harpsichord—the keyboard being covered with a cloth— with as much facility as if he could see the keys.

"He will instantly name all the notes played at a distance, whether singly or in chords, on the harpsichord or on any other instrument, bell, glass, or clock. He will finally improvise as long as may be desired, and in any key, on the harpsichord and the organ."

As he matured, Mozart's reputation as a composer soon rivaled his fame at the keyboard. He produced an avalanche of compositions: symphonies, operas, chamber music, concerti, masses, and songs, all of which seemed to flow effortlessly from his pen. He would generally work out the details of his composition in his head, and later write down the notes onto paper in astonishing time. His barber even complained about the difficulty of dressing Mozart's hair—the composer would constantly be getting an idea and dash to the keyboard, with the barber in hot pursuit. Explaining his enormous artistic energy, Mozart answered simply, "Composition is less tiring than doing nothing."[1]

Mozart's genius attracted attention throughout Europe. It produced a number of jealous rivals who did their best to discredit him. But it also won him many friends, notably the great Haydn from Esterhazy. After hearing several of Mozart's string quartets, Haydn exclaimed to the composer's proud father, "I assure you before God, as an honorable man, your son is the greatest composer that I know personally or by reputation." These beautiful quartets Mozart later dedicated to his "*caro amico* Haydn".

Mozart was also perceptive in recognizing the talent of others. When a brash, young and unknown musician named Beethoven insisted on playing for the celebrated Mozart, the latter was very impressed. He turned to his friends nearby and uttered a prophetic remark: "Keep your eyes on him. Someday he will give the world something to talk about." Years later, Beethoven would return the compliment, writing in 1826, "I have always reckoned myself among the greatest venerators of Mozart, and I shall remain so until my last breath."

The spiritual life of this great Austrian composer has often been overlooked. Despite notorious portrayals by a few modern writers and movie makers, the true picture of the man emerges from his personal letters — and hundreds have been preserved — from recollections of those who knew him, and from the work of serious musicologists. Mozart possessed an unusual, multi-faceted personality which bears little resemblance to contemporary caricatures of him.

Mozart remained childlike throughout his short life. Carefree and confident, he loved games, dancing and masque balls. He had almost no financial sense, which led to disaster when money was scarce, but this was partly born out of his intrinsic generosity. When a fellow composer's illness kept him from fulfilling a commission and endangered his salary, Mozart completed the work by his friend's bedside, taking no credit for its composition. At another time, Mozart was accosted by a beggar in the streets of Vienna. Having no money to give, he brought the man to a coffee-house, quickly wrote down an entire Minuet and Trio, gave them to the man with a letter, and sent him to his publisher. The astonished panhandler soon possessed five *guineas.*

For the most part, Mozart's life reflects a moral reputation and a steadfast faith in God. Friedrich Kerst, one of the editors of the composer's published letters, states, "Mozart was of a deeply religious nature.... Mozart stood toward God in a relationship of a child full of trust in his father." [2]

Mozart's parents were pious Catholics, and their son developed a sincere, personal relationship to Christ. Mozart's faith stayed intact even when he came under attack by corrupt churchmen. The most notorious example of this was the heartless Archbishop of Salzburg, who belittled Mozart, impaired his career, and one day had the musician physically tossed out of his cathedral.

Most of Mozart's correspondence is light-hearted and witty, and it is true that one set of letters written to a young cousin sinks to indecency. But this is the rare exception, though it has been popularly capitalized upon.

One of the dozens of letters the composer wrote to his father details his sensitivity to spiritual matters and his reliance on God: "Papa must not worry, for God is ever before my eyes. I realize His omnipotence and I fear His anger; but I also recognize His love, His compassion, and His tenderness towards His creatures. He will never forsake His own. If it is according to His will, so let it be according to mine. Thus all will be well and I must needs be happy and contented." [3]

Concerning his personal morals, Mozart writes, "I cannot possibly live like the majority of our young men. In the first place, I have too much religion, in the second too much love for my fellow men and too great a sense of honor..." [4] He assured his worrisome father that, "I know that I have so much religion that I shall never be able to do a thing which I would not be willing openly to do before the whole world."[5] He once cancelled a tour with two musicians of ill-repute, noting that, "Friends who have no religion are not stable."[6]

As a 14-year-old, Mozart reported that he prayed every day, and he wrote requests for prayer from Christians around him.[7] Even some of his compositions, such as the great *Mass in C Major*[8] and the *Davidde Penitente,*[9] were the result of sacred vows he had made privately with God.

Prayer accompanied a major part of Mozart's life. When his father expressed concern over Mozart's upcoming marriage, Mozart answered that he and Constance shared a unique spiritual compatibility. He insisted, "I found that I never prayed so heartily, confessed or communicated so devoutly, as when by her side. And she feels the same."[10]

The Mozarts had a loving and steadfast marriage, strong enough to withstand the attacks aimed at them by Mozart's critics in Vienna. Scandalous tales of Mozart's womanizing have long since been discounted. Constance, although as financially inept as her husband, was a faithful helpmate to Mozart as he worked.

On many late nights, Mozart would pore frantically over his musical scores by candlelight, while Constance attended him. She prepared his favorite punch, and amused him with stories and jokes while he composed, to help him stay awake.

Toward the end of his life, Mozart joined a Freemason lodge in Vienna. It should be noted that modern Masonic institutions have evolved considerably from those social gatherings of the eighteenth century, which included such members as Samuel Wesley and George Washington.[11] Katherine Thomson, in her inclusive study of the Masonry of that period, insisted that for Mozart it was certainly not "inconsistent for a Freemason to be a Christian."[12] The musicologist Alfred Einstein even suggested that Mozart's attraction to Masonry was primarily for social reasons. He wrote that, "Perhaps he was driven into the Lodge by his feeling of profound loneliness as an artist and his need for unreserved friendship."[13]

Mozart's faith was deeply personal. It bore the marks of Roman Catholicism, Protestant influence, eighteenth century Enlightenment thinking, and the Freemason movement, yet it was authentically Christian. His true faith was based on a private relationship between himself and Christ.

Mozart's letters are often punctuated with expressions of faith and praise to God, as well as concern for the spiritual lives of those around him: "It will greatly assist such happiness as I may have to hear that my dear father and my dear sister have submitted wholly to the will of God, with resignation and fortitude—and have put their whole confidence in Him, in the firm assurance that He orders all things for the best."[14]

While hoping to receive an appointment from Elector Karl Theodore in 1777, Mozart wrote, "Let come what will, nothing can go ill as it is the will of God; and that it may so go is my daily prayer."[15] The following year, he tells of the success of a new symphony: "I prayed to God for His mercy that all might go well, to His greater glory, and the symphony began."[16]

When a friend was seriously ill, Mozart comforted his mother and sister: "You should not grieve too deeply, for God's will is always the best. God will know whether it is better to be in this world or the other."[17] After the composer's beloved mother died, he wrote, "By a singular grace of God I endured all with steadfastness and composure. When her illness grew dangerous I prayed God for two things only - a happy hour of death for my mother, and strength and courage for myself. God heard me in His loving kindness, heard my prayer and bestowed the two mercies in largest measure."[18]

His faith concerning the issues of life and death shows strong conviction. "I believe, and nothing shall ever persuade me differently, that no doctor, no man, no accident, can either give life to man or take it away; it rest with God alone."[19]

At age 31, Mozart may already have had premonitions about the brevity of his own life. His reflections, at this age, indicate a mature Christian commitment: "I never lie down in my bed without reflecting that perhaps I— young as I am—may not live to see another day; yet none of all who know me can say that I am socially melancholy or morose. For this blessing I daily thank my Creator and wish it from my heart for all my fellow men."[20]

Just four years later, at age 35, Mozart died. His health, which had always been frail, at last failed him while he worked in poverty on his last great masterpiece, the *Requiem.*

His biographer, Otto Jaun, has summarized the consensus of history, when he calls this Mozart's *Requiem,* "The truest and most genuine expression of his nature as an artist. It is his imperishable monument."[21] A contemporary of Mozart writes, "Mozart has disclosed his whole inner being in this one sacred work, and who can fail to be affected by the fervor of devotion and holy transport which streams from it? His *Requiem* is unquestionably the highest and best that modern art has to offer for sacred worship."[22] The composer's expressive treatment of the centuries-old Latin text clearly reveals his strong faith in "The Lamb of God, who takes away the sins of the world."

At one point, Mozart confessed to Constance that he believed death was near and that he was writing *Requiem* for himself.[23] Racked with pain on his deathbed, and surrounded by several friends, the composer sang the alto part at an informal rehearsal of the unfinished work. During the "Lacrimosa" movement, Mozart burst into tears, and his final rehearsal ended.[24] He died early the next morning, December 5, 1791. His last action was to imitate the kettledrums in his *Requiem.*

Mozart left behind not only an unparalleled legacy of musical treasure, but a record of eighteenth century faith. A genius such as Mozart possessed, developed so fully in so young a man, may have tempted others to spiritual indifference. Mozart leaves evidence of a different response. He wrote in a letter, "Let us put our trust in God and console ourselves with the thought that all is well, if it is in accordance with the will of the Almighty, as He knows best what is profitable and beneficial to our temporal happiness and our eternal salvation."[25]

SOME THOUGHTS ON MOZART: ENTHUSIASM

It has often been said that the difference between a successful man and a failure is not the number of problems each may have, but the fact that the successful man takes action to overcome his problems. Mozart was a man of action and enthusiasm. The many volumes of his compositions show us that he spent his 35 years achieving, not content to sit and rest on the laurels of a childhood career.

Mozart was a sensation as a prodigy, yet as a man he was surrounded by depressing misfortunes. The very genius that could have resulted in success caused intense jealousy among rival composers, some of whom openly worked for Mozart's ruin. He was never given the well-paid position which he obviously deserved. His last decade was a continual struggle against poverty for himself and his dearly beloved family. If he had been inclined to discouragement, he had enough affliction to completely paralyze his musical output.

Yet his response was the very opposite of paralysis. When the pressures of money mismanagement were overpowering him, Mozart would tear headlong into a brilliant new composition. When he saw other composers winning the public and denouncing his works, he would begin anew, writing innovative works that would eventually eclipse his competitors' best efforts. A lesser man might have allowed his bitter predicaments to stifle his imagination, but Mozart sustained his enthusiastic drive even through the debilitating suffering of his last year.

Ultimately, generations have received the benefit of thousands of Mozart's works because he simply refused to be a slave to the circumstances around him. When he obtained a commission he quickly fulfilled the request. But even when he went without such an incentive, he continued to create masterpieces, such as his last great symphonies, composed without commission or even the prospect of an upcoming performance.

His stupendous number of compositions proves that action is the best remedy for discouragement. As long as he could compose, he was incapable of despair. His indefatigable spirit—which was cultivated as a successful prodigy—had taught him to find his motivation internally, with or without the impetus of praise from others.

RECOMMENDED LISTENING:

Orchestral Music: 41 Symphonies, notably No. 40, in G minor and No. 41, in C major, "Jupiter"; Eine kleine Nachtmusik, for strings.

Chamber Music: 23 String Quartets, notably the 6 "Haydn" quartets; 2 piano quartets; Quintet in A major, for clarinet and strings.

Keyboard: 21 Piano Sonatas, notably Sonata in A Major, K. 331.

Choral Music: Requiem; Ave Verum Corpus.

Operas: The Marriage of Figaro; Don Giovanni; The Magic Flute.

"In whatsoever
manner it be,
let me turn
to Thee
and
become
fruitful
in good works."

5

LUDWIG VAN
BEETHOVEN
1770 - 1827

An opera rehearsal is under way, and the singers and orchestra members focus closely on their conductor. He gestures wildly as the musicians struggle to interpret his intent. What could he possibly want them to do? Two violinists exchange furtive glances, commiserating wordlessly about how difficult it is to work with such an idiosyncratic composer and conductor.

The music deteriorates into a cacophony of random notes, then falls helplessly silent. Yet the conductor seems confused, obviously unaware of the reason for the rehearsal's breakdown. The sight of this man's horrified face points toward only one conclusion, the musicians gradually realize. He is deaf, and he is trying valiantly to conceal his deafness.

Who will put a stop to this travesty? The embarrassed musicians shift awkwardly in their chairs, staring at their instruments or at one another and not daring to look at the conductor. The conductor scrutinizes the instruments in the laps of the musicians and studies their mortified faces. He summons a friend to his side, and the friend scribbles a note: "Please do not go on; more at home."

The conductor reads the note hastily, then turns on his heels and races out of the opera hall. He does not stop running until he reaches his home, where he throws himself on the sofa and buries his face in his hands. For hours, Ludwig van Beethoven remains in a devastating state of depression, no longer able to hide the loss of his hearing from the world.

Ludwig van Beethoven, considered by many the greatest composer who ever lived, was a devoted admirer of Handel and his music. On his death bed, he claimed, "Handel is the greatest, cleverest composer. From him I can still learn." It is no wonder Beethoven felt a special kinship with his predecessor; both men continued their artistic endeavors in the face of great adversity. Handel struggled against an intermittent series of external misfortunes, however, while Beethoven's conflict was internal.

From the time he was born in 1770, Beethoven faced overwhelmingly difficult circumstances. His alcoholic father proved irresponsible and harsh, and his loving mother remained frail and sickly until her death at age 40. Beethoven's talent for music presented itself when he was a young boy, yet his father was not successful at exploiting it in the same way as Mozart's father.

When he was a young man, Beethoven moved to Vienna, the musical capital of Europe, and began performing for the nobles who gathered there. His virtuosity at the piano made him extremely popular with the aristocracy, even when his crude manners left them aghast. Beethoven's mannerisms and general appearance were notoriously rough and clumsy, yet he was not the least bit intimidated by his refined patrons. He made no attempt to impress them or to change his uncultured ways.

A disheveled Beethoven frequently took long walks in the countryside. Once, at the height of his fame, a police officer mistook him for a tramp as he wandered outside the city of Baden. Placing him under arrest, the officer must have smiled indulgently in disbelief as Beethoven loudly protested, indignantly declaring his identity. He would have spent the night in jail, but a local musician came to his rescue, identifying the unkempt derelict as the great Beethoven.

Beethoven matured at a time when all of Europe was in an uproar. Revolution was in the air, all forms of establishment were being challenged, and Napoleon was on the march, relentlessly conquering every nation in his path. At first, Beethoven admired the might of this new conqueror and planned to dedicate his third symphony to him. But when he learned that Napoleon had proclaimed himself Emperor, Beethoven flew into a rage and tore up the title page. The composer's stormy life is marked by many such outbursts, triggered by events large and small. Once, at a restaurant, a waiter mistakenly brought him the wrong order. An enraged Beethoven hurled the dish and food into the very face of the flustered servant.

He had many devoted friends, yet Beethoven's life was characterized by loneliness and misunderstanding. He remained a bachelor, though not by choice. He proposed to several different women, all of whom admired his genius but clearly perceived that his erratic personality would make him an intolerable husband.

The defining tragedy of his life, and the one which diminished his performing career, was his growing deafness. The pain and humiliation he experienced because of it drove him almost to suicide. In 1802, he poured out his heart in a letter to his brothers, saying deafness meant he "must live as an exile."[1]

Beethoven wrote, "It was impossible to say to others: 'Speak louder; shout! For I am deaf.' ... How great was the humiliation when one who stood beside me heard the distant sound of a shepherd's pipe, and I heard nothing—or heard the shepherd sing, and I heard nothing. Such experiences brought me to the verge of despair."[2]

It was this miserable affliction, and not malice toward others, that intensified the tumultuous eruption of emotion which is found throughout Beethoven's life and music. A friend once watched in anguish while the former master pianist attempted to play piano in a rehearsal of his *Archduke Trio*. It turned out to be one of the last times Beethoven ever played his instrument for anyone. After hearing the pathetic attempt, Beethoven's friend wrote, "If it is a great misfortune for any one to be deaf, how can a musician endure it without giving way to despair? Beethoven's continual melancholy was no longer a riddle to me."[3]

In his famous *Heiligenstadt Testament,* the deaf composer gave voice to his deepest longings: "Almighty God, you look down into my innermost soul, you see into my heart and you know that it is filled with love for humanity and a desire to do good."[4] Indeed, Beethoven could be altruistic and sympathetic to the affliction of others. When he learned that Bach's only remaining daughter was in need, he immediately offered to publish a new work for the elderly woman's exclusive benefit.

As Beethoven's deafness increased, he withdrew more and more into the work of composing and into his intimate and unorthodox relationship to God. Beethoven lived until 1827. On his deathbed he reassured his brother of his "great readiness" to make his peace with God.[5] One of the last acts of his life was to receive communion.[6] Beethoven's friend, Anselm Huttenbrenner, remained with the composer at his death, which took place during a violent storm. Following a loud clap of thunder, Huttenbrenner wrote, the unconscious Beethoven awoke, "opened his eyes, raised his right hand, his fist clenched, and looked upward for several seconds with a grave, threatening countenance, as if to say, 'I defy you, powers of evil! Away! God is with me!'"[7]

Discerning Beethoven's beliefs is no easy task. All of his biographers agree that he was intensely spiritual,[8] and his close friend, Anton Felix Schinder, insists that Beethoven's "entire life is proof that he was truly religious at heart."[9] But his untraditional faith makes it difficult to categorize the composer.[10] Beethoven, like many geniuses, was a very complex man with eclectic interests and influences.

Beethoven was born and baptized into a Roman Catholic family. His mother, it is reported, was very pious, and young Beethoven was sent to a Catholic school. There, as he commented later, he was brought up "with proverbs" by a Jesuit teacher.[11] In his youth he attended a variety of churches, and his principal teacher and mentor, Christian Gottlob Neefe, was a Protestant believer.[12]

Beethoven's diaries, letters, and conversation books (with which he communicated after he was deaf) contain dozens of devout references to God, giving evidence of strong conviction. In a typical spirit of forceful certitude, he wrote, "It was not a fortuitous meeting of chordal atoms that made the world. If order and beauty are reflected in the constitution of the universe, then there is a God."[13]

His relationship to God was deeply personal, and he turned to God to make sense out of life's unfairness: "Therefore, calmly will I submit myself to all inconsistency and will place all my confidence in your eternal goodness, O God! My soul shall rejoice in Thee, immutable Being. Be my rock, my light, forever my trust!"[14] In 1815, he even expressed his hope of finding tranquility and fulfillment in composing for "a small chapel" where he would dedicate his works to "the glory of God, the Eternal."[15]

Throughout his diary, ardent prayers appear:[16] "In whatsoever manner it be, let me turn to Thee and become fruitful in good works."[17] To a close friend in 1810, he confessed an almost child-like faith. He wrote, "I have no friend. I must live by myself. I know, however, that God is nearer to me than others. I go without fear to Him, I have constantly recognized and understood Him."[18] To his friend, the Grand Duke Rudolf, Beethoven wrote, "Nothing higher exists than to approach God more than other people and from that to extend His glory among humanity."[19]

Beethoven owned both a French and a Latin Bible[20] and, at least late in life, he prayed with his young nephew every morning and evening.[21] His library included such Christian devotionals as Thomas a Kempis' *The Imitation of Christ*[22] and a very heavily marked copy of Christian Sturm's *Reflections on the Works of God in Nature,* the work of a Lutheran minister.[23] "Socrates and Jesus have been my models,"[24] Beethoven wrote in a conversation book of 1820. His devotion was simple and private. In a letter to a friend, he commented, "Today happens to be Sunday, so I will quote you something out of the Bible, 'See that ye love one another.'"[25]

And of course, Beethoven composed some of the most profound Christian masterpieces of history. The most notable of these include his oratorio *Christ on the Mount of Olives,*[26] which seems to embody Beethoven's identification with the suffering savior; the *Mass in C,* which Beethoven termed "especially close to my heart";[27] and his monumental *Missa Solemnis,* considered by many to be the greatest Mass ever composed. His *Gellent Songs,* Opus. 48, were settings of religious poems, prayers and a psalm. These were not commissioned, but were freely chosen by the composer because of his affinity for their spiritual texts.[28]

Beethoven's spiritual convictions show themselves even in his musical sketches. In the manuscript of his String Quartet No. 15, he writes, "Song of Thanksgiving to God on the recovery from an illness, in the Lydian Mode."[29] In the sketches of the *Pastoral Symphony,* he wrote, "Oh Lord, we thank thee."[30] For years Beethoven showed a preoccupation with the Church modes. In 1809 he wrote, "In the old church modes the devotion is divine...and God let me express it someday."[31] He contemplated composing a choral symphony, describing it as "a pious song in a symphony, in the old modes; Lord God, we praise thee, alleluia."[32]

Nevertheless, other aspects of his life seem to contradict this picture. Although Beethoven was born a Roman Catholic, he never practiced this faith.[33] He had a marked suspicion of priests and avoided going to church.[34] His brash personality seemed, outwardly at least, to prevent Christian charity from being recognized. Beethoven had a strong interest in Eastern literature, and he even copied three Hindu passages which he kept under glass on his desk.[35] He had no scruples whatsoever in quoting pagan verse, such as the famous "daughter of Elysium" from the *Ninth Symphony.* "Elysium" originated as a pagan name for heaven.[36] That Beethoven believed in the Christian religion cannot seriously be doubted, but his personal faith embraced idiosyncratic interpretations that go well beyond the rituals of the typical churchgoer.[37]

Beethoven's complex personality traits leave the world's greatest musicologists at odds on the subject of the composer's faith. Perhaps the best clues to his personal beliefs can be found in Beethoven's music—music which reveals the man himself. Evidence of Beethoven's serious, searching approach to matters of faith may be found in his greatest sacred work, *Missa Solemnis*. For this composition, Beethoven took unprecedented pains with his research, studying the history of church music, gathering hymn manuscripts from local monasteries,[38] even obtaining a new and more accurate translation of the Latin so every word would be fully understood.[39]

He wrote at the top of the score, "From the heart—may it go to the heart."[40] Possibly the cornerstone of *Missa Solemnis* is the movement "Dona nobis pacem," over which he inscribed, "A prayer for inner and outer peace."[41] This is the peace that Beethoven sought all his life and found, it would seem, if only at his death.

SOME THOUGHTS ON BEETHOVEN: DETERMINATION

The portrait of Beethoven's life which emerges from historical accounts, his own written reflections, and his music is one of tremendous achievement in the face of unimaginable difficulty and tragedy. He confronted a physical affliction which not only was constant and worsening, but one which caused him shame, humiliation and disgrace. Yet he refused to succumb to the dejection created by his deafness. Year after silent year he continued to compose masterpieces which actually increased, rather than abated in musical excellence.

Today, in a world marked by medical and technological advances as well as public awareness and acceptance of physical defects, it is difficult to grasp the devastating nature of the obstacles Beethoven faced. Now there are unobtrusive and effective hearing aids, worn with no more thought of shame than a common pair of glasses. But if Beethoven wanted to hear at all, he had to hold up a bulky, cumbersome ear-trumpet. This not only exposed his abnormality to everyone around him, but also attracted the cat-calls of street urchins and delinquents in Vienna.

Hearing loss such as this would present a severe trial to anyone, but for a musician—indeed, a master musician—deafness was devastating. Beethoven wrote, "Alas! How could I possibly refer to the impairing of a sense which in me should have been more perfectly developed than in other people, a sense which at one time I possessed in the greatest perfection, even to a degree of perfection such as few in my profession possess or have ever possessed—oh, I cannot do it."

Nevertheless, Beethoven was determined to prevail and to continue in his art, which he considered a sacred trust placed upon him by his Creator. The very strength and resolve which piqued others to call him brusque and tactless enabled him to continue and even to expand his natural compositional gifts. It is astonishing to study the complexities and beauty of his late works and to realize that, except in his imagination, he never heard them performed.

Beethoven's principle virtue was his sheer determination to overcome, although this often obscured the many other virtues he possessed. The judgment of a man's greatness is not only to be measured in the mission he accomplishes, but in the obstacles he has overcome in the process. Not only was the genius of this deaf eccentric recognized by his contemporaries, thousands of whom lined the streets of Vienna at his funeral, but also in the universal veneration of every subsequent musical age.

RECOMMENDED LISTENING:

Orchestral Music: Nine Symphonies, notably No. 3 ("Eroica"), No. 5, No. 6 ("Pastoral"), and No. 9 ("Choral"), Five Concerti for Piano, notably No. 55 ("Emperor"), Concerto for Violin.

Chamber Music: 16 string quartets, notably No. 14 in c# minor.

Piano Music: 32 Piano Sonatas, notably No. 8 ("Pathetique"), and No. 14 ("Moonlight").

Choral Music: Missa Solemnis, Mass in C, Christ on the Mount of Olives.

Opera: Fidelio.

"It sometimes
seems to me
as if
I did not
belong
to this world
at all."

6

FRANZ PETER
SCHUBERT

1797 - 1828

Seeking some diversion from his work, the young composer stops in at a favorite Vienna cafe. It's a bit shabby, but caters to a fascinating variety of artists and vagabonds. As his eyes adjust to the dim candlelight, he makes his way toward a group of friends gathered at a small table and settles down comfortably among them. He digs into his pockets and finds there is not enough money for a glass of wine. He contents himself with a cup of coffee.

To take his mind off pressing thoughts of unpaid debts and poor health, the composer thumbs through a German edition of Shakespeare's *Cymbeline*. The lively chatter of his friends begins to quiet as they catch a gleam in the composer's eye. He reads aloud the words of a poem in the Shakespeare play that begins, "Hark, hark, the lark." A lovely melody comes to mind, and the composer insists he must write it down.

But the cafe is quite dark, and there is no paper. One of his friends grabs a menu and scratches down some staves on the back of it. The composer sets to work, scribbling rapidly in the dim light. Within moments, his work is completely finished.

That evening the composer, Franz Peter Schubert, and his friends gather around the piano. His new composition, one of the most beautiful songs of the nineteenth century is performed for the first time.

The short life of Franz Schubert is a study in incongruity. Known for so many beautiful and joyful compositions, he encountered a doleful succession of disappointments, anguish and poverty. Born in Vienna to a penniless schoolmaster and his wife, Schubert never received a thorough musical education. His talents were so abundant, however, that in 1808, at age 11, he was accepted as a chorister in the court chapel. A few years later he began to compose. He persevered even when he was so poor he could not afford music paper; the only paper he owned for composing was given as a gift.

When his voice broke in 1813, Schubert (like Haydn 64 years earlier), was abruptly dismissed from the court chapel. Discouraged and disheartened, he worked for three joyless years in his father's school. Then he embraced an unconventional, happy-go-lucky existence and stayed with it for the rest of his life. Fortunately, his cheerful disposition won him a great number of friends, some of whom formed a musical clique called the Schubertians. These were not rich patrons who could solve his financial problems, but they did encourage him to compose many of his greatest masterpieces.

Schubert spent most of his life destitute and struggling, but financial hardship never diminished his enthusiasm to compose. It is astonishing to see how many hundreds of compositions came pouring out of his imagination—songs, symphonies, chamber music, masses and piano works—dozens of which are considered standard repertoire today. He stated, "When one piece is finished, I begin another." Schubert even went to bed with his glasses on so he could begin working as soon as he awoke!

Sadly, his music brought the composer almost no income whatsoever. In 1823, his remarkable song *The Erl-King* became very popular and finally secured him considerable earnings. But he carelessly sold the rights to this classic for the equivalent of a few hundred dollars. He sold a publisher twelve volumes of his songs for 800 *florins;* from just one of these, the *Wanderer,* the publisher profited over 36,000 *florins.*

Another time, Schubert completed two orchestra movements and sketched two more, then he dropped the project and sent the manuscript away. One of his friends retrieved this score in 1865, and as a result Schubert's *Unfinished Symphony* was finally premiered. It continues to be one of the most celebrated musical fragments in history.

Personal tragedy compounded Schubert's difficulties, particularly after he befriended a young man named Franz Schober. Removed from his father's guiding influence, Schubert was, in the words of other friends, "led astray" by this irreligious man. Few details remain of their escapades in the Vienna nightlife, but most scholars today believe Schubert contracted syphilis as a result.

Theatre managers continually refused to stage Schubert's operas, and the relentless strain of rejection darkened the composer's optimistic temperament. He worked occasionally for the family of Count Esterhazy, but most of the local music posts he desired and felt he deserved went to other composers.

Schubert's great hero was Beethoven. Although they have scarcely met, Beethoven had studied some of his songs and proclaimed, "Truly in Schubert dwells a divine spark!" The younger composer deeply grieved when his hero died, and he carried a torch in Beethoven's funeral procession. Within two years Schubert himself lay dying, in a delirious fever diagnosed as typhus, the common disease of the city slums. He was only 31 years old.

Schubert's short life passed in relative obscurity, and many details about his thoughts and beliefs remain unknown. Yet it is evident that his personal faith in God served to strengthen his spirits against oppressive hard times. His close friend Anselm Huttenbrenner wrote, "Schubert had a devout nature and believed firmly in God and the immortality of the soul. His religious sense is also clearly expressed in many of his songs. At the time when he was in want he in no way lost courage, and if, at times, he had more than he needed he willingly shared it with others who appealed to him for alms."[1]

Schubert's baptismal certificate affirms that his parents were both "believers in the Catholic religion,"[2] and they appeared to be particularly devout. A young friend once reminisced about Schubert's consideration toward others, saying it "showed that his mother had laid the foundation of religious feeling and uprightness with great care and motherly tenderness, filling his youthful heart with these."[3]

His father's faith is evident in a consoling letter he wrote to his other son, soon after the composer's untimely death. In it, the father exhorts him to "seek comfort in God, and to bear any affliction that may fall on us according to God's wise dispensation with resolute submission to His holy will. And what befalls us shall convince us of God's wisdom and goodness, and give us tranquillity. Therefore take courage and trust implicitly in God. He will give you strength, that you may not succumb, and will grant you a glad future by His blessing."[4]

Schubert's education, if musically inadequate, at least encouraged his spiritual growth. When he joined the chapel choir, he gained admittance to the Imperial and Royal City Seminary and consequently to its clerical lectures.[5] Biographers note that when his old music teacher Papa Holzer encouraged Franz to write him some church music, "the boy did not need much urging."[6]

A long poem by Schubert on the subject of God's omnipotence is mentioned by his friend Anton Holzapfel. Unfortunately, the poem has been lost.[7]

His friend Huttenbrenner recalled asking Schubert "whether he did not also want to try setting prose to music and chose, for this purpose, the text from St. John, Chapter VI, verse 59: 'This is that bread which came down from heaven: not as your fathers did eat manna and are dead: he that eats of this bread shall live for ever.' He solved this problem wonderfully in twenty-four bars, which I still possess as a very precious souvenir of him. He chose for it the solemn key of E major and set the above verse for a soprano voice, with figured bass accompaniment."[8]

Schubert referred to his faith in his letters, thanking God for his talents.[9] In 1825, he wrote home describing the way his audience responded to a new sacred work he had composed. It "grips every soul and turns it to devotion," he wrote. Concerning his audience, he remarked that they "wondered greatly at my piety."[10] He concluded, "I think this is due to the fact that I have never forced devotion in myself and never compose hymns or prayers of that kind unless it overcomes me unawares; but then it is usually the right and true devotion."[11]

Other letters reveal different sides of his character. In one he humorously solicits funds from his brother with the biblical quote, "Let him that hath two coats give one to the poor."[12] In another, he deplores certain music which "engenders in people not love but madness: which rouses them to scornful laughter instead of lifting up their thoughts to God."[13] In still another, he explodes with revulsion at the sight of a cross and a chapel which were raised to observe the sight of a bloody battle. "These sacred symbols are intended partly to commemorate and partly to expiate a horrible crime. Oh, dear Christ, over how many deeds of shame must Thou lend Thy countenance? Of Him who in Himself is the most convincing testimony to own human wickedness, they erect an image everywhere in wood and stone, as much as to say, 'See here, we have trampled under our profane feet the most perfect creation of the great God. What shall hinder us then in annihilating easily the rest of ordinary mankind?'"[14]

In 1816 Schubert began to keep a diary, noting odd thoughts that occurred to him in solitude: "Man comes into the world with faith, which is far superior to knowledge and understanding, for in order to understand a thing one must first of all believe in it. Reason is nothing more than analyzed belief."[15] Mired in poverty, he once wrote, "A man endures misfortune without complaint, but he feels it the more acutely. Why does God endow us with compassion?" Another time he wrote, "The world resembles a stage on which every man is playing a part. Approval or blame will follow in the world to come."[16] His day-to-day difficulties may have turned Schubert's longings toward God. "It sometimes seems to me as if I did not belong to this world at all," he observed.[17]

But it is Schubert's music itself which reveals the composer's faith most clearly. His biographer Peggy Woodford notes that, despite our lack of many details concerning Schubert's life and beliefs, all of his music presupposes "an intense spiritual life."[18] His songs in particular, she writes, "imply that he was a deeply religious man."[19]

Musicologist Carl A. Abram, writing about the last of Schubert's great Masses, states, "Certainly it is impossible to doubt the heartfelt piety and God-fearing humility which shines through even the most extended and turbulent of all the Masses, namely, the E-Flat major. Only a truly religious spirit could prompt Schubert to have the chorus cry out utterly alone, as though from the wilderness of despair, at the beginning of the *Gloria*. Only an inner longing for divine help and release could have sustained the brooding and melancholy Schubert of the last years (the Mass was composed in the last six months before his death) in the long, imploring sob, eleison, which occurs shortly before the end of the *Kyrie*. ...this Mass is undeniably an expression of strong religious devotion."[20] The composition moved Oskar Bie to write, "It is the song of Christ's incarnation. The whole choir bears the crucifixion."[21]

Victory over death is a main theme in all the Schubert *Novalis* settings, according to renowned baritone Dietrich Fischer-Dieskau. In a study of Schubert songs, he wrote, "Schubert's struggle with this phenomenon is manifested here as the personal experience of an act of faith."[22] Schubert wrote a considerable amount of sacred music, notable for its diversity. Among these works are his Hymn to *Faith, Hope and Charity,*[23] the sacred cantata *Miriam's Song of Victory,*[24] and the *Hymn to the Holy Spirit*, over which the composer appears to have taken great pains.[25] Furthermore, Schubert left behind an unfinished Easter cantata based on the biblical account of Jesus raising Lazarus from the dead.[26]

Schubert was raised Catholic, yet he wrote music for other churches, especially in his later years.[27] He even omitted the words, *Credo in unam sanctam catholicam it apostolicam ecclesiam* ("I believe in one holy Catholic and apostolic church") from his Masses.[28] For years, he longed for a *Kapellmeister* post where he might work for a local church,[29] but such an offer never materialized.

Perhaps because he was never confined by a job to a specific church, his spiritual life was as individualistic and personal as his musical gifts were unique and self-taught. Through the tribulations of his tragic life, it was the combination of two elements in his nature—his faith in God and his God-given talent—which enabled him to create without applause or acclaim the many masterpieces we treasure today.

SOME THOUGHTS ON SCHUBERT: SINCERITY

Listening to Schubert's music, especially the hundreds of beautiful songs that flowed from his pen, the simple sincerity of the composer's soul is evident. His music is transparent and is seldom mistaken for works of any other composer. He refused to look upon his talent as a tool for making money. Rather, he poured out his heart into every work.

Dietrich Fischer-Dieskau, famed for singing Schubert Lieder, has said, "No matter how great our admiration for Schubert may be, we (those who perform his songs) only realize later in life what it is that raises him far above the level of other composers: Schubert is *authentic*." Schubert never affected false pretenses, either in his music or in his life. No wonder he made many friends. Those around him believed they really knew the whole man, without reservation, and they were right. In the stuffy, ostentatious society of Vienna, such openness and simplicity must have been a breath of fresh air.

In retrospect, Schubert clearly made mistakes in his life that inevitably resulted in devastating consequences. Yet in his principle calling, to be an original and innovative composer, he refused to compromise. Doubtless he could have achieved greater financial success writing trite nonsense for the multitudes. For Schubert, this would have been flagrant duplicity.

The immediate price for this sincerity was far greater than the absence of universal fame: it resulted in a life of impoverishment. But the fruit of this sacrifice is still being appreciated by generations who have loved the beauty and simplicity of Schubert's many works. Had this composer been anything less than sincere, he may have opted to seize immediate gratification. Instead, he chose the way of integrity, and we reap the rewards of his legacy.

RECOMMENDED LISTENING:

Orchestral Music: Nine Symphonies, notably Symphony No. 8, in B minor, "Unfinished"; Symphony No. 9, "The Great", in C major.

Chamber Music: Quartet in A minor; Quartet in D minor, "Death and the Maiden"; Quintet in C major, for strings; Quintet in A major, for piano and strings, "Die Forelle".

Piano Music: Moments musicaux; Impromptus; Sonata in C minor.

Vocal Music: More than 600 songs, including "Erlkonig," "Die Forelle," "Tod und das Madchen," "Ave Maria," "An die Musik," "Gretchen am Spinnrade," "Heidenroslein."

"Pray to God that He may create in us a clean heart and renew a right spirit within us."

7

FELIX
MENDELSSOHN

1809 - 1847

The visitor arrives late, tapping at the door almost imperceptibly in case the family is asleep. When no one answers, he lets himself in and makes his way toward his friend's music study. He knows it well from engaging in many friendly dialogues there that have continued long into the night.

As he enters, he sees his friend engrossed in his Bible. The visitor stands quietly, awkwardly, for a moment. Finally, the master of the house glances up at the visitor, showing no sign of surprise and offering no greeting. "Listen," he says, and excitedly begins to read aloud: "And behold, the Lord passed by...." He reads on and on, his voice rising in pitch as the drama of the passage overwhelms him.

The visitor recognizes the story of Elijah, when suddenly the reading stops. "Would not that be splendid for an oratorio?" asks Felix Mendelssohn, setting the Bible on his desk and searching his friend's face for a reaction. Thus the greatest oratorio of the nineteenth century was conceived.

Many of the great composers seem to have suffered more than their share of life's misfortune and frustration. In sharp contrast, Felix Mendelssohn led, for the most part, a happy and successful life. Born into a wealthy and cultured family, his remarkable talents were encouraged from the start, and he brilliantly pursued an abundance of musical endeavors.

Rather than producing a spoiled cavalier, his cultivated upbringing gave Mendelssohn a sensitive and charitable spirit. In a typically benevolent frame of mind, he wrote a friend, "I dislike nothing more than finding fault with a man's nature or talent; it only depresses and worries and does no good; one cannot add a cubit to one's stature, all striving and struggling are useless there, so one has to be silent about it, and let the responsibility rest with God."[1]

His grandfather, Moses Mendelssohn, had been an important Jewish philosopher, yet the composer's father Abraham was somewhat uncertain in his beliefs.[2] At first, he raised his children "without religion in any form,"[3] though his brother-in-law was strongly influencing him toward Christianity.[4] In those times Jews encountered deep prejudice throughout Europe. Only with the greatest difficulty had the Mendelssohn family acquired a degree of wealth.

Once when he was a child, Mendelssohn ran home in tears from chorus practice. The chorus had been singing a passage from Bach's *St. Matthew Passion* when another youth hissed mockingly, "The Jew-boy raises his voice to Christ!" Seeing his children tormented because of their religious heritage was too much for Abraham; a desire for his children's happiness rather than personal spiritual conviction finally persuaded him to have them baptized and raised in the Christian faith.[5]

Yet Mendelssohn, far from resenting his forced entry into the new faith, embraced it fervently his entire life.[6] In his manuscripts this young prodigy often penned a prayerful exclamation: *Lass es gelingen Gott!* ("Let it succeed, God!") or *Hilf Du mit* ("Help along").[7] His biographer, Eric Werner, writes, "He was faithful to the Christian religion and took it seriously.[8] ...Reverence, fear of God, the sense of praise, of gratitude, of bitter complaints and of pride in one's faith, all these lay in his personality. He had great respect for the Biblical Word."[9]

When he matured, Mendelssohn joined the Lutheran church, although he attended worship services of various denominations. At one point, he inclined toward Catholicism, but his passionate love for the music of the Protestant Bach anchored him to Lutheranism.[10]

One of Mendelssohn's many illustrious accomplishments was to "redis-cover" and champion Bach's music, which had become neglected and all but forgotten. He considered Bach's work "the greatest Christian music in the world."[11] In fact, he held one particular Bach chorus in such high regard that he wrote, "If life had taken hope and faith from me, this single chorus would restore all."[12] From the time he was a boy badgered for his Jewish roots, he was spellbound by the *St. Matthew Passion*. He and a friend from the theater mounted it in a full performance, after decades of obscurity. When Mendelssohn mounted the podium to conduct, he found that a different musical score had been mistakenly placed in front of him. He conducted the entire composition by memory, even turning the pages of the incorrect score, to not alarm the unknowing soloists. His devotion to the Baroque master initiated the grand "Bach revival" of the nineteenth century.

Mendelssohn excelled as a composer, a pianist, a conductor, and the founder of the Leipzig Conservatory of Music. Not that his life was always idyllic; he ran into a number of personality conflicts as a conductor and administrator. But his talent won consistent acclaim, and his acquaintances included the finest musical geniuses of Europe: Schumann, Liszt, Wagner, Paganini, Weber and Chopin, to name a few.

Mendelssohn never hesitated to display his faith openly to those around him. Fellow composer Berlioz, a radical free thinker, once recalled, "Mendelssohn believed firmly in his Lutheran religion and I sometimes shocked him profoundly by laughing at the Bible."[13] Another fellow composer later recorded his admiration of Mendelssohn: "So richly favored and endowed, so beloved and admired, and at the same time so strong in mind and character, that he never once let slip the bridle of religious discipline, nor the just sense of modesty and humility, nor ever fell short of his standard of duty."[14] His wife, Cecile, the daughter of a well-known clergyman of the French Reformed Church,[15] was a pious believer and a woman of prayer.[16]

For Mendelssohn, the Bible served as the cornerstone of daily life as well as the inspiration for much of his work. When he set passages of Scripture to music, he was painstakingly precise about the wording.[17] According to a friend who knew him well, "He felt that all faith must be based on Holy Writ."[18] Mendelssohn congratulated his librettist, noting "I am glad to learn that you are searching out the always heart-affecting sense of the scriptural words."[19] When the biblical text was altered, Mendelssohn observed, "I have time after time had to restore the precise text of the Bible. It is the best in the end."[20]

Mendelssohn's letters reveal a profound faith in God.[21] Echoing the words of a psalm, he wrote, "Pray to God that He may create in us a clean heart and renew a right spirit within us."[22] To his nephew, he wrote, "Nothing is attained, without the fulfillment of one fervent wish—May God be with you! This prayer comprises consolation and strength, and also cheerfulness in days to come."[23]

His own work as a composer blended his belief in divine inspiration with his Protestant work ethic. "I know perfectly well that no musician can make

his thoughts or his talents different to what Heaven has made them; but
I also know that if Heaven had given him good ones, he must also be able
to develop them properly."[24] He composed a great deal of sacred music,
notably his celebrated oratorios *Elijah* and *Saint Paul*. The story of Paul's
dramatic conversion to Christianity touched Mendelssohn deeply. As he
composed it, he wrote, "I must not make any mistakes."[25] His letters speak
of a holy zeal to complete the project,[26] and in the process he devoured
everything he could read on Greek and Church history, as well as daily life
in the time Paul lived.[27]

Mendelssohn's music is universal in its appeal, and his compositions
run the gamut from "Ave Maria" to texts of Martin Luther set to music.[28]
He felt dissatisfied with music created by many Catholic composers,
observing, "I have found, to my astonishment, that the Catholics, who
have had music in their churches for several centuries, and sing a musical
Mass every Sunday if possible, in their principle churches, do not to this
day possess one which can be considered even tolerably good, or in fact
which is not actually distasteful and operatic.... Were I a Catholic, I would
set to work at a Mass this very evening; and, whatever it might turn out,
it would at all events be the only Mass written with a constant remem-
brance of its sacred purpose."[29]

Mendelssohn demonstrated a careful authenticity in composing
sacred music, and the same trait is evident in his personal views on how
the Christian faith should be interpreted and lived. Once, he found
himself the object of praise by members of the "heavenly minded" Pietist
movement. He responded, "So I am said to be a saint! If this is intended
to convey what I conceive to be the meaning of the word, and what your
expressions lead me to think you also understand by it, then I can only say
that, alas! I am not so, though every day of my life I strive with greater
earnestness, according to my ability, more and more to resemble this
character. I know indeed that I can never hope to be altogether a saint,
but if I ever approach to one, it will be well.

"If people, however, understand by the word 'saint' a Pietist, one of
those who lay their hands on their laps and expect that Providence will do
their work for them, and who, instead of striving in their vocation to press
on towards perfection, talk of a heavenly calling being incompatible with
an earthly one, and are incapable of loving with their whole hearts any
human being, or anything on earth, then God be praised! Such a one I
am not, and hope never to become, so long as I live. And though I am

sincerely desirous to live piously, and really to be so, I hope this does not necessarily entail the other character."[30]

Mendelssohn's life was cut short after he received the crushing news that his sister and close companion had suddenly died. He lost consciousness and fell, rupturing a blood vessel in his head. He never recovered, remaining very ill until his death a few months later at the age of 38. Even when he knew death was approaching, he cheerfully and steadfastly maintained his faith. Mendelssohn wrote, "A great chapter is now ended, and neither the title nor even the first word of the next is yet written. But God will make it all right one day; this suits the beginning and the end of all chapters."[31]

SOME THOUGHTS ON MENDELSSOHN: OPTIMISM

Mendelssohn's life was particularly happy and successful, especially in comparison with so many other composers. Furthermore, Mendelssohn maintained a very positive attitude toward life, full of optimism, confidence, and expectation for the future. The question then arises: Did his good attitude develop in response to all the splendid circumstances in his life, or did the splendid circumstances arise because of his optimistic attitude?

Whatever the outcome of such a debate, one thing is clear: Mendelssohn's positive outlook was an invaluable asset. He expected excellent results and he generally got them, even in some very large-scale musical ventures. He expected to be a world-class musician, and he became one even in his teens. He expected the world to react enthusiastically to his "rediscovery" of Bach's music—and it did, and still is! He expected to get a principal conducting post, and in his mid-twenties he was given Leipzig's prestigious Gewandhaus Orchestra. He expected to create a great music school, and in 1843 founded the renowned Leipzig Conservatory of Music. He even expected to have a passionate, loving marriage with Cecile, and he did; historical accounts indicate their "love story" could have provided the script for a romantic novel.

Of course, none of these accomplishments came without effort. Mendelssohn's own teacher remained skeptical about the first Bach performance. Before he gained the Gewandhaus position, Mendelssohn had to endure the frustration of directing a miserable musical season at Dusseldorf. And before the Conservatory could take shape, he struggled to obtain not only the permission but the financial backing of an indifferent king.

Yet it seems Mendelssohn never gave a thought to the possibility of failure. He knew what he wanted to do, and he resolved to see it done. His name was quite appropriate: Felix in Latin means "happy man." He lived his life as though he considered this name a prophetic gift. Not that he dealt in bravado or exulted in applause; his quiet confidence gave him an unassuming and modest temperament. He simply expected to be successful, and his accomplishments in 38 years offer convincing proof of the benefits of his optimism.

Recommended Listening:

Orchestral Music: Five Symphonies, notably No. 4, ("Italian") and No. 5, ("Reformation"); Concerto in E minor, for violin and orchestra; A Midsummer Night's Dream, suite; Fingal's Cave ("Hebrides") Overture.

Chamber Music: Octet in E-flat major.

Piano Music: Songs Without Words.

Oratorio: Elijah, St. Paul.

Choral Music: Psalms; Hymn of Praise.

"Through Christ alone, through resigned suffering in God, salvation and rescue come to us."

8

FRANZ
LISZT
1811 - 1886

The music emanating from the piano fills the room with
exquisite sound. A hushed audience sits spellbound, as if they were
in the presence of a seasoned master musician. Yet before their eyes
is a 12-year-old boy, his legs stretching to reach the pedals beneath
the piano and his smooth face furrowed in close concentration.

He appears almost at one with the instrument he plays, striking
the keys with a remarkable combination of authority and sensitivity. Not since Mozart have the concert goers of Vienna seen such
a prodigy. They exchange hurried glances of approval and disbelief.

When the music stops, the audience thunders its applause. A
man awkwardly steps toward the piano as a whisper makes its way
throughout the hall: the great Beethoven is here. Even though he
is almost completely deaf, Beethoven recognizes the rare talent
before him. He sweeps the boy up in his arms and kisses him on
the cheek. For the rest of his life, the moment remains seared in the
memory of the boy, Franz Liszt. Within months, Liszt would be
proclaimed by the public to be the "eighth wonder of the world."

The Age of Romanticism produced many contradictions in art, politics
and religion. It was a time of emerging self-expression and individualism, and
a time of breaking new ground, expanding musical horizons. Innovation

marked the Romantics, and so did sentimentality. Few individuals personified these incongruities more completely than the pianist-composer Franz Liszt. His imaginative career generated a host of legendary events. Scholars are still at odds over the authenticity of such incidents as that described above, even though it was described by Liszt himself. His many-sided personality defies easy analysis, and it is particularly difficult to reconcile his devout spirituality with his outrageous lifestyle.

On one hand, Liszt was a fervent Christian all his life and even entered the priesthood when he was in his fifties. On the other hand, he was an incorrigible womanizer who careered from one glamorous affair to another, often with women who appeared to share his sincere religious outlook on life. Above all, he was a master musician—possibly the greatest virtuoso of his century—who from boyhood dazzled the adoring audiences of Europe. These internal inconsistencies wrestled within him throughout his long and colorful life.

"From youth up, Franz's spirit was naturally inclined to devotion, and his passionate feeling for art was blended with a piety which was characterized by all the frankness of his age," reads an entry in the diary of his father, who died when Liszt was 16.[1] As a child, Liszt's favorite reading materials included the Bible, St. Thomas a Kempis's *Imitation of Christ*, and the lives of the saints. Hungering for stories about the lives of the apostles, he begged his mother to read from the Bible. The narrative of Christ's Passion moved him to tears, and the simple ceremony of bedtime prayer brought him great comfort and joy.[2]

Liszt's consuming interest in Christianity made him long to enter the priesthood, and he frequently implored his parents to enroll him in seminary.[3] His parents, both devout Catholics, instead chose to encourage his musical career. Once when Liszt persisted in talking about becoming a priest, his father brought him up short: "You belong to music, not to religion. Love God, be good and honest, and you will reach the highest summits in art, a vocation for which the natural gifts Providence has bestowed upon you have destined you."[4]

Undeterred, Liszt's passion for God intensified. At age 17, he pleaded tearfully, once again, to be allowed to enter the Paris Seminary: "I hoped it might be granted to me to live the life of the saints and perhaps die the death of the martyrs."[5] Even his mother, who gave him a strong sense of religion and duty,[6] was troubled by the raw emotion of his letters. He later wrote to her, "You know, dearest mother, how during the years of my youth, I dreamed myself incessantly into the world of the saints. Nothing seemed to me so self-evident as heaven, nothing so true and so rich in blessedness as the goodness and compassion of God."[7]

Yet despite all his religious fervor, Liszt led a life of epic sensual self-indulgence. Throughout most of his adult life, Liszt participated in a series of celebrated love affairs. He became intimate with well-known and highly placed women such as the Countess Marie d'Agoult and the Princess Carolyne Sayn-Wittgenstein, a wealthy patron remembered for her mystical religiosity and her incessant cigar smoking![8]

Much has been written already about this composer's long romances, with so little emphasis on his faith. And it is true that Liszt never married, even after living for years with one lover or another and fathering several illegitimate children. Liszt showed no outward sign of embarrassment or guilt over his affairs, and he appeared rather indifferent to the opinions and the censure of others.[9] Yet living in a state of blatant contradiction between belief and action could not be completely dismissed. He appeared painfully aware of the inconsistencies of his life, however, which caused persistent inner turmoil and periods of depression.[10]

Thwarted in his youthful ambition to become a priest, Liszt found in music an outlet to express his faith as well as his extraordinary talent. His renown as a virtuoso pianist made him the most sought-after musician in Europe. As a performer, a composer, and a teacher, he profoundly influenced other musicians of his day. Yet Liszt also believed he had a calling to compose church music. Writing to a friend in 1856, he claimed, "I have taken a serious stand as a religious, Catholic composer. Among the composers I know, none has a more intense and deeper feeling for religious music than your humble servant."[11]

Liszt pondered the future of church music, writing in an article, "The church composer is also preacher and priest and where words cannot suffice to convey the feeling, music gives them wings and transfigures them."[12] Biographer Eleanor Perenzi observes, "Liszt was probably the nineteenth century's greatest composer of religious music, alone in his blend of scholarship, originality and devotion."[13] Another biographer, van Wessem, wrote, "Liszt has never done anything without profound religious thought."[14]

As early as 1834, the composer himself insisted that music's purpose was, "to ennoble, to comfort, to purify man, to bless and praise God."[15] Liszt composed many works of sacred music, both in choral genre, such as his settings of five psalms, masses, and oratorios; and in such piano pieces as the *Harmonies poetiques et religieuses,* the two *Legendes* and the last book of the *Annees de pelerinage.*

A particular depth of inspiration appears evident in his spiritual compositions. Concerning his *Solemn Mass,* he wrote Wagner that he had "prayed this

Mass rather than composed."[16] Liszt composed his *XIIIth Psalm* "weeping blood," as he subsequently wrote.[17] In his last decades he was intrigued with the influence of the Gregorian chorale, as seen in such works as his *Via Crucis*.[18] For his greatest religious work, the massive oratorio *Christus*, Liszt wrote his own Latin libretto composed of extracts from the Holy Scriptures.[19]

The religion of this romantic was not a thoughtless, superstitious trust in a *"Genie-God"* but a firm faith in the deity who created the universe and remains active in it. Concerning this balance between stark rationalism and unpredictable mysticism, he writes that he "knew neither ecstasy nor visions."[20] He makes it clear that his beliefs are firmly rooted in conventional Christianity: "The ardent longing for the Cross, and the elevation of the Cross have always been my true, my innermost vocation."[21]

One person who distinctly influenced the composer was the Abbe de Lamennais, a devout writer who attacked the excesses of the Catholic Church and became one of the most prominent ministers in Europe. Liszt spent hours in fellowship with this man who loved the arts and God. The Abbe once wrote, "God is the greatest artist, his work is the world."[22] Their admiration was mutual: Liszt called Lamennais "fatherly friend and instructor,"[23] and the Abbe wrote Liszt that he would "glory and be proud to be one day called your disciple."[24] The musicologist Hugh Reginald Hawais, who knew them both, claimed it was Lamennais "who, more than any other, saved Liszt from drifting into the prevailing whirlpool of atheism."[25]

Letters Liszt wrote contain many references to his faith as well as his concern for others. In a letter to the younger composer, Richard Wagner, who later became Liszt's son-in-law, he wrote, "I will pray to God that he may powerfully illumine your heart through His faith and His love. You may scoff at this feeling as bitterly as you like. I cannot fail to see and desire in it the only salvation. Through Christ alone, through resigned suffering in God, salvation and rescue come to us."[26]

To Princess Marie zu Sayn-Wittgenstein he wrote, "May God keep you and lavish His blessings upon you. I will yet add what is said in the Gospel for Whitsunday: 'Let not your heart be troubled, neither let it be afraid.' Jesus gave you His peace—not as the world gives it."[27] In another letter, he writes encouragingly, "Carry out, then, with devout confidence, the inspiration of your heart, and the Lord's blessing be upon all upright souls."[28] In still another, he comforts: "Even on the most troubled days, there is certain peace for those who have the single felicity to be Christians."[29] Like the grand finales of many of his compositions, Liszt's letters often ended with a flourish: "May God be with you and may we love each other through Him, in this life and for Eternity!"[30]

Perhaps Liszt found the inner reconciliation he needed when, on April 25, 1865, he entered the Third Order of St. Francis of Assisi in Rome and became Abbe Liszt. Later in life he confessed, "If it had not been for music I should have devoted myself entirely to the church and would have become a Franciscan; it was my most innermost wish which led me to join the church that I wished to serve."[31]

Liszt considered his ordination the most important event of his life,[32] and he made elaborate preparations for it. He withdrew for a few days to the monastery of the Lazzaristi, and in a journal, he recorded how he spent his days. He rose from bed at half-past six, meditated alone in his cell, drank coffee in his room, attended Mass at half-past eight and, on Sundays, High Mass at half-past nine. Then came solitary Scripture readings, visits to the Holy Sacrament, and dinner in the refectory at midday, where he ate alone at a little table, unfortunately too far away from the pulpit to hear the readings given by a monk. In the afternoon, he walked in the garden, read the Bible, and spent one hour in solitary meditation. Supper was served at eight o'clock in silence, and religious discussions with the Superior followed until half-past nine. Lights out occurred at ten o'clock.[33]

After a glamorous career as the world's greatest pianist, Liszt plunged into a life of startling austerity. At times, his experience in the priesthood must have seemed humiliating. After only ten days as an Abbe, Liszt had to practice his genuflexions for almost three hours at the command of a religious superior.[34] But far and wide, people still appreciated Liszt. Even the Pope himself admired and loved Liszt, calling him "his dear son" and "his Palestrina." The Pope even told him that the law "ought to employ your music, in order to lead hardened criminals to repentance. Not one could resist, I am sure."[35]

Nevertheless, Liszt's life did not end in Rome. After a few years of seclusion, he began to travel, teach piano students, and occasionally even perform. All the proceeds of his concerts went to charity, not personal gain. As late as 1874, he turned down an offer for an American concert tour which would have guaranteed him 600,000 francs. Liszt remained an enigma to his last day, flirting with his students while in his seventies, yet maintaining throughout his life that he was "a true believer."[36]

Every six months, Liszt "consecrated a week to the salvation of his soul," one friend recalled.[37] Once on Good Friday, he spent the whole afternoon and the following day in church. On his knees before the image of Christ, Liszt cried unreservedly and smote his breast.[38] Two days later, on Easter Sunday, Liszt was overheard speaking to a woman with whom he had been romantically associated. Perhaps he summed up the spiritual and emotional struggles he endured when he told her: "You see, my dear, there's nothing like putting your conscience in order."[39]

SOME THOUGHTS ON LISZT: GENEROSITY

Accounts of the lives of great artists frequently dwell at length on details of their shortcomings. Portraying an artist's personal failings is easier — and more popular—than appraising the nobler virtues that may invite emulation. Certainly the composer Liszt had his share of imperfections, especially in the extramarital category, which cannot be excused. Yet biographers consistently note that as a man, he was never hated. Rather he was respected, loved and admired—and not merely for his talent. There was sound reason for this: Liszt possessed some exemplary personal virtues that should not be overlooked.

Ultimately, Liszt was a great philanthropist, giving liberally of his funds and his service to those in need. As a young man, his earnings went to pay his father's debts and to support his mother. At the height of his career, with potential millions right at his fingertips, he renounced giving concerts for money. Once he raised huge sums in Russia, for example, then he gave every cent to charity. His concerts also raised a small fortune for a "pension for destitute musicians." Hearing that a Beethoven Memorial was being planned, he immediately volunteered to help and paid for most of it himself. He had sacrificed so many of his worldly goods by 1865 that when he entered the Order of St. Francis, he possessed nothing but "his cassock, a little linen, and seven handkerchiefs."

Liszt was altruistic in other ways as well. Throughout his life he supported the music and careers of many other composers, often at his own expense. When he was appointed to an influential position of *Kapellmeister* in Weimar, he unselfishly programmed concert after concert championing the music of other composers rather than his own. Once, when Liszt heard that very few tickets were bought for an upcoming concert of Wagner's music, he volunteered to perform a Beethoven concerto on the program. The result was an immediate sell out.

Dozens of Liszt's piano pieces are actually his transcriptions of the works of others. This gave other musicians a greater opportunity to present their music to the public, which was a crucial need in the days before recorded music. And

Liszt supported many composers financially, giving and loaning liberally, often without expecting to be repaid—particularly in the case of Wagner.

As the private teacher of a generation of pianists, Liszt refused to be paid for his invaluable lessons. The immense amount of time freely invested into his pupils would later yield an abundant musical harvest through such men as Von Bulow, Weingartner, Albenez, Bizet, Moszkowski, Joachim, Rosenthal, Smetana and Saint-Saens, among others. And without the encouragement he gave to countless musicians, perhaps many of the great romantic compositions would not be in the repertoire today.

When the life of Franz Liszt is measured in terms of all he contributed to others, the extent of his generosity is astounding. Even with all his faults, he is a striking example of a life of consistent benevolence. Rarely has a man been so unselfish toward others, and rarely has a man had such a powerful impact on his times. In the case of Liszt, these two factors are inseparable. His influence continues to be appreciated today, endowing the present generation not only with his own music, but also the music of the many musicians he inspired.

RECOMMENDED LISTENING:

Orchestral Music: Les Preludes; Faust Symphony; Dante Symphony; Piano Concerto No. 1 and No. 2.

Piano Music: Hungarian Rhapsodies; Liebestraum; Annees de Pelerinage; Sonata in B minor.

Organ Music: Fugue on the Name of B.A.C.H.

Masses: Missa Choralis; Hungarian Coronation Mass.

Choral Music: Christus; Psalm 13; Psalm 116; Psalm 128.

"*Christianity's founder was not wise, but divine.... To believe in Him, meant to emulate Him: to hope for redemption, to strive for union with Him.*"

9

RICHARD
WAGNER

1813 - 1883

It is August 1876, and the small Bavarian town of Bayreuth hums with unprecedented activity and anticipation. From all around the world, famous composers, members of the nobility, and devotees of music are gathering, crowding the inns and jostling townspeople in packed cafes. Animated talk all through the town centers on a single subject: a musical premiere and the place where it will be staged.

The event has been long in the making. For the past twenty years, the composer has developed and polished a single work consisting of more than ninety different themes and requiring more than twelve hours to perform. And over the past five years, a massive fundraising effort has finally succeeded in financing an imposing new theatre, built exclusively for this composition.

At last, August 13 arrives. Tchaikovsky, Liszt, Saint-Saens and a host of other composers settle into their seats while members of the aristocracy fill a special "Prince's Gallery." As they await the beginning of the monumental work, members of the audience thumb through an exhaustive "guidebook," attempting to comprehend the scope of a four-opera cycle of music which will be performed over the course of four days.

Members of the orchestra take their places, and the theatre falls quiet. A triumphant Richard Wagner exults as the first notes of his magnificent *Ring of the Nibelung* fill the concert hall.

Anyone who is acquainted with Richard Wagner's life and work may wonder why he is present in a book about spiritual life. Wasn't he known for his self-centeredness, for pursuing outrageous love affairs, and for befriending the philosopher Nietzsche, the self-styled "anti-christ" and Christian-hater?[1] Wasn't Wagner later idolized by Hitler as a prophet of the Third Reich?[2]

Before closing the book in disgust, — wait and see. There is a side of this musical genius that few have ever acknowledged and which deserves careful consideration. At the same time, there is no excuse for his undeniably shameful actions and views. Approaching an understanding of his life that makes room for some ambivalence does not require us to condone the whole man.

As a boy, the brilliant Wagner showed an early affinity for literature, culture and different languages, but never for music. Not until he reached his teens— after being inspired by Weber and Beethoven—did young Wagner study music. Then, as he did everything in his life, he rushed into it with reckless abandon. He rushed into marriage as well, proposing to an actress named Minna Planer just after he began his musical career at age 20.

Wagner and his wife made one another miserable through three decades of dire poverty. Yet through it all Wagner kept on producing musical masterpieces—works which would go unheard and unappreciated for many years. Once, the Vienna Court Opera agreed to produce Wagner's new work *Tristan and Isolde*. Each singer struggled to learn the difficult music, and then struggled further to get through the confusing rehearsals. No one had ever seen such bizarre music, such complexity, such gibberish. Before Wagner could witness the composition's premiere, the opera's frustrated director finally shelved the work as unplayable, after giving it a full *seventy-seven* rehearsals!

A crucial turning point came in 1864 when one of Wagner's few great admirers, Ludwig II, ascended to the throne in Bavaria and became Wagner's "super-patron." The new king magnanimously paid all of Wagner's debts and gave the composer a generous salary. Now, Wagner's wildest dreams could become reality. The compositions he created mark the birth of an entirely new genre of musical form, which he called the "music drama." Chief among his accomplishments is the monumental *Ring of the Nibelung* and the mammoth Bayreuth theater built to stage it.

After Wagner's first wife died, he ignited a roaring scandal by wooing the brilliant Cosima Von Bulow, wife of Hans Von Bulow, a noted conductor and devotee of Wagner's music. The Von Bulow's marriage was annulled conveniently, and Wagner married Cosima, which did result in a happy marriage. The composer continued to produce extraordinary works, both in music and literature, until his death at the age of 69.

Wagner's musical genius stands uncontested, yet his spiritual views form a bewildering assortment of inconsistencies.[3] To begin with, he was a sensitive and impressionable child. He wrote in his autobiography that as a boy he "gazed with agonized sympathy" on the crucifix of his church,[4] and "yearned with ecstatic fervor to hang upon the Cross in place of the Saviour."[5] But the poor examples of his local clergymen soon dampened his fervor,[6] and for years the spiritual influences around him were negligible. Yet there are hints of a growing interest in Christianity. Once, he announced he would compose a heroic opera on the life of Martin Luther.[7]

Moreover, the 36-year-old Wagner startled his friends when he embarked on a huge work entitled *Jesus of Nazareth*, saying he was "inspired by a study of the Gospels."[8] His associates flatly discouraged this ambition. Wagner later wrote that the pessimistic philosopher Bakunin, learning of the composer's project, "insisted that I must at all costs make Jesus appear as a weak character."[9] Wagner nevertheless worked for months on the libretto, producing a dramatic harmony of the Gospel accounts.[10] It contained extensive sketches including dozens of other New Testament verses.[11] With no chance of support, the relatively unknown Wagner finally abandoned what could have been an important sacred work.

Still later, he completed a gargantuan work for orchestra and three choruses entitled *The Love Feast of the Twelve Apostles*.[12] The writing displays a clear understanding of the biblical text and perhaps even a measure of devotion to it. Performing the work required 1,200 singers and 100 instruments, and its premiere overwhelmed Wagner himself. He later wrote, "The Holy Ghost was poured out upon my *Love Feast of the Twelve Apostles* and we were all transported."[13]

Christian themes emerge clearly in some of Wagner's music dramas, such as *Tannhauser, Lohengren,* and his last great work, *Parzival,* which has been called his "most Christian of works."[14]

As early as 1848, Wagner found himself compelled to address an insistent internal longing for transcendant meaning in life. He wrote, "When I found this yearning could never be stilled by modern life, and realized once again that redemption was to be had only in flight from this life, in escaping from its claims upon me by self-destruction, I came to the primal fount of every modern rendering of this situation—to the man Jesus of Nazareth."[15]

Yet what about his friendship with Nietzsche? It would seem that they were friends only until they really understood one another.[16] In 1876, they met for the last time. Wagner's acceptance of Christianity angered his colleague,[17] who deserted him and later denounced him hysterically in his article, "The Fall of Wagner."[18] Nietzsche wrote, "Incredible, Wagner has turned pious."[19] He bitterly assessed his former friend's conversion by observing, "Richard Wagner, apparently the most complete of victors, fell suddenly, helpless and broken, before the Christian cross."[20]

Wagner's personal faith appeared to be growing. In 1880, he wrote a lengthy article "Religion and Art," in which he calls Jesus Christ, the "all-loving Saviour," who was "born to suffer and die for mankind, redeeming the human race through His blood."[21] Wagner professed belief in the divinity of Jesus,[22] the virgin birth,[23] the validity of Christ's miracles,[24] and a literal interpretation of his Second Coming, which he believed would follow the fall of man's political systems.[25]

This composer looked forward to the world's spiritual future: "We await the fulfillment of Christ's pure teaching...the son of the Galilean carpenter, who preached the reign of universal human love—thus would Jesus have shown us that we all alike are men and brothers."[26]

Wagner wrote that Christ's blood, "was a fountainhead of pity, which streams through the human species."[27] The only hope for the world, Wagner concluded, was the true Christian sacrament, "partaking of the blood of Christ."[28] Concerning Jesus, the composer wrote, "Christianity's founder was not wise, but divine....To believe in him, meant to emulate him: to hope for redemption, to strive for union with him."[29]

Is it surprising to read these quotes? Unfortunately, they tell only half the story. In fact, if Beethoven's Christianity could be considered "unorthodox," Wagner's interpretation is far more so. He utterly rejected the Old Testament, stating that "The Christian God has been erroneously identified with the Jewish tribal god: the god of punishment and war, not the redeeming Saviour of the poor."[30] He dismisses the Ten Commandments as lacking any trace of Christian love.[31]

Many of Wagner's religious views seem to be colored by his apparent anti-Semitic feelings.[32] These odious views were influenced strongly by his associates, especially the French philosopher Count Gobineau.[33] Perhaps this aspect of Wagner's life has been exaggerated in this century, in reaction against Adolf Hitler's devotion to his music. Hitler was a vile maniac and a thoroughly unartistic man who neither understood Wagner nor his music.[34] Actually, Wagner surrounded himself with Jewish friends and supporters, notably

Rubinstein, Neumann, and his superb conductor Levi.[35] Wagner urged his conductor and friend to be baptized into the Christian faith, yet he openly admired the man's conviction for remaining steadfast in his Judaism.[36] In a letter to his father, a Rabbi, Levi defends Wagner against the charge of anti-Semitism. Levi speaks warmly of their mutual love and admiration.[37]

The great irony of Wagner's peculiar and inconsistent views about Christianity, of course, is that his acknowledged Savior was a Jewish carpenter sent to the lost sheep of Israel. This presented no problem for Wagner. With the sure conviction of the self-deluded, he swept history aside and wrote, "It is more than doubtful if Jesus himself was of Jewish extraction."[38] He made the baffling "discovery" that Jesus was born "among the silent vegetarian communities founded by Pythagoras."[39] Vegetarianism was another one of Wagner's favorite hobby-horses. For instance, he claimed to have discovered that the Last Supper was an exhortation to vegetarianism,[40] mistranslating Jesus' words: "Taste such alone, in memory of me."[41]

These and many other bizarre ideas leave one wondering whether this musical genius was otherwise mentally deficient.

Was Wagner a Christian? He would have insisted upon it indignantly, at least at some points in his life. But there are few Christians who would not be repelled by his outlandish and unsupportable beliefs. That he had an intense spiritual life cannot be doubted. But the emotions and opinions it produced are, at best, stupefying. The contradictory life of this great composer has bewildered musicologists for decades, and continues to do so.

SOME THOUGHTS ON WAGNER: PERSEVERANCE

If ever a man had to persevere singlehandedly through years of relentless failure, it was Wagner. For three solid decades, until Ludwig II came to his rescue, the composer experienced more rejection personally and musically than any other master in written history. Even Handel in England could celebrate an occasional success to balance his array of difficulties. For Wagner, life was a uninterrupted series of defeats, forcing him to move constantly from town to town, but never eliciting surrender.

After failure and rejection from the *Thomasschule,* he was barely accepted into the University. Soon, his first opera was rejected at Leipzig, and his second was withdrawn after a fiasco in Magdeburg. He was hired as a conductor in Konigsberg, and the company immediately went out of business. Finding another conducting job in Riga, he was soon fired and had to elude frontier guards to escape his creditors. In Paris, a new opera company of his failed, and he actually spent time in a debtor's prison. Finally, he had a "hit" opera (*Rienzi*) in Dresden, but even this proved a financial calamity. Although it brought immediate cash and a good job in Saxony, news of Wagner's success traveled swiftly to his many creditors throughout Europe. They pounced upon him, demanding huge sums of money he still could not pay.

By this time, his marriage was in ruins, debts continued to mount, and he frequently fell ill, needing expensive medical treatments. Wagner's next few operas flopped. Then he narrowly escaped being thrown in jail when he foolishly joined a political rebellion, which forced him to flee into Switzerland. Yet, at a time when he desperately needed to write works that could bring quick money, he was determined to pursue the composing of his mammoth *Ring* cycle. He labored on it tirelessly, fully aware that even if he lived to complete the project, he would surely never have the funds to see it produced.

How could he have kept going? It would seem that Wagner refused to acknowledge the concept, "impossible." The defeats he encountered would have crushed the strongest of temperaments, yet he continued to create music that redefined an entire art form. It took years for some of his works to gain acceptance, but now he has an almost cult-like following throughout the world. His music is not for everyone, but those who cherish it are often fanatical zealots who spend a fortune each year flying from around the globe to experience the Bayreuth festivals. It may not always be easy to appreciate his compositions, much less his peculiar beliefs. Yet it is impossible to feel anything but awe for a man of such unshakable perseverance.

RECOMMENDED LISTENING:

Orchestral Music: Siegfried Idyl.

Opera: Tannhauser; Lohengrin; Tristan und Isolde; Die Meistersinger; The Flying Dutchman; The Ring of the Nibelungs (The Rhinegold, Siegfried, The Valkyries, and The Twilight of the Gods); Parsifal.

Choral Music: The Love Feast of the Twelve Apostles.

"I study
with the birds,
flowers, God,
and myself."

10

ANTONIN DVORAK

1841 - 1904

The riotous commotion of New York City bewilders the Bohemian maestro, arriving there in 1892. In the three years he spends directing the National Conservatory of Music, he vacillates between exploration and retreat. There are times when he wanders to the railway station, awed by the mammoth steam engines and the rushing, chattering crowds. And there are times when he rejuvenates himself alone in Central Park, tossing bread crumbs to flocks of pigeons and drinking in the all-too-rare sight of trees and grass.

Eager to get in touch with the music of this strange, vibrant country, this composer learns from a black American music student the beauty of Negro spirituals. This music conveys ecstatic joy and deep sorrow so effectively that it brings tears to the maestro's eyes.

In the summertime, he feels extremely homesick for his native Prague. Friends persuade him to take the train to rural Spillville, Iowa, where the composer delights in spending time with a community of fellow Bohemians. There, the variegated sights and sounds of America continue to fascinate him. Sitting outdoors on a summer evening, he listens intently as three Iroquois perform traditional Indian music.

In the rural tranquility of Spillville, the composer takes time to sift all the images and impressions that have bombarded him since he arrived. He soon begins work on a new composition. The result is one of Antonin Dvorak's greatest and most celebrated symphonies, entitled *From the New World.*

Present-day Czechoslovakia was known as Bohemia when Antonin Dvorak was born there on September 8, 1841. His parents struggled continuously to make ends meet, and they feared their son's musical ambitions were a sure ticket to continued poverty. Even though they loved music and appreciated the boy's phenomenal talent, they told their crestfallen son that an education in music was out of the question.

Yet Dvorak dedicated himself to his calling as a musician, leaving home and working himself through Prague's Organ School. Each day when he left the school, he faced a difficult challenge: his musical studies were hampered because he could not afford even to rent a piano, much less buy one. He recalled later that these were years of "hard study, occasional composing, much revision, a great deal of thinking, and very little eating." Against all the odds, Dvorak became—and remains—the greatest composer of his nation's musical history.

In Prague, Dvorak spent time with many talented musicians. When he was 22, Dvorak played viola in an orchestral concert of Wagner's music, conducted by the composer. This experience affected him deeply, and for several years his youthful compositions reflect Wagner's influence. But as a composer he remained virtually self-taught: "I study with the birds, flowers, God, and myself."[1]

At the beginning of his career Dvorak met the famous composer Johannes Brahms, who became a close friend and strong supporter. Brahms convinced his publisher to distribute Dvorak's music, and he influenced musicians throughout Europe to play the young composer's works. By his mid-forties, Dvorak's fame was well-established. His musical career would span the globe, with performances from Vienna, Austria to Chicago, Illinois. When he died in 1904, his native Bohemia declared a day of national mourning.

National and international acclaim did not alter Dvorak's simple and humble nature. In no way did he fit the stereotype of the eccentric composer. He cherished his wife and many children and savored their company even as he composed. Instead of retreating to the solitude of a private study, Dvorak often worked at the kitchen table. Surrounded by the aroma of bread baking in the oven and the din of children chasing noisily through the house, Dvorak did some of his best composing.

A revealing picture of Dvorak's home life is given by a student who recalled, "His children were permitted to invade his studio at all times, even while the composer was at serious work. My daily lessons were usually taken with the accompaniment of grimacing boys and girls hidden behind articles of furniture, or appearing at unexpected moments in doorways out of their father's sight."[2]

Throughout his life, Dvorak maintained a reputation of character, high morals, and great faith.[3] He spoke of his genius as "the gift of God" or as "God's voice."[4] When writing about his colossal *Mass in D Major,* he characteristically proclaimed, "Faith, hope and love to God Almighty and thanks for the great gift of being enabled to bring this work in the praise of the Highest and in the honour of art to a happy conclusion." Then he added, "Do not wonder that I am so religious. An artist who is not—could not produce anything like this. Have we not examples enough in Beethoven, Bach, Raphael and many others?"[5]

Dvorak's relationship to God appears to have been consistently reverent and personal.[6] His principle biographer, Otakar Sourek, notes that an unchanging feature of Dvorak's nature was his "sincere piety."[7] The composer loved reading the Bible and owned copies in English as well as modern and ancient Czechish.[8] Dvorak's letters are full of spiritual observations, and his manuscripts regularly began with the marking "With God" and ended with the benediction, "God be thanked."[9] When he traveled, he wrote letters to his children encouraging them to go to church often and "pray fervently."[10]

Once, while working with a librettist on his opera *Rusalka,* he observed that a character was supposed to say, "I curse both God and spirits all." This troubled Dvorak immediately, and he asserted, "Listen, I am a believer. I can't curse God in my music."[11] When he first met Anton Seidl, conductor of the New York Philharmonic Orchestra, Dvorak was horrified at the man's blasphemous speech and his irreligious beliefs, yet he continued to befriend the conductor.[12] His beloved friend Brahms, though not an agnostic, distressed Dvorak because of his lack of simple faith. A person who listened in on a long conversation about religion between the two composers later noted, "On the way back to the hotel, Dvorak was more than usually silent. At last after some considerable time he exclaimed with emotion, 'Such a man, such a soul—and he doesn't believe in anything, he doesn't believe in anything!'"[13]

He viewed his extraordinary composing skills as being inspired by God, claiming that he would "simply do what God tells me to do."[14] Dvorak's sacred music reveals the portrait of a devout soul. Musicologist Mosco Carner writes,

"Religious music was to him a means to express in the first place *his* feeling of devotion, *his* idea of the Deity."[15]   He sometimes used parts of old Czech hymns and plain-chant melodies,[16] but would often blend the holy texts with lively dance themes from his native Bohemia. As biographer Gervase Hughes aptly notes, "Consequently it was not unnatural that Dvorak should set the opening lines of the *'Credo'* to a melody that would have served equally well for a graceful waltz, and having thereafter treated the references to Christ's crucifixion and death in a mood of deep seriousness he saw nothing in-congruous in bursting once again into a somewhat perfunctory jog-trot at the word *'et resurrexit.'* "[17]

Dvorak's beautiful *Stabat Mater* is considered by many to be his greatest work.[18] The music was set to the poem by Jacopone di Todi, and in it the grief of Jesus' mother echos Dvorak's own grief at the loss, within a short time, of three of his children.[19] His exquisite *Biblical Songs,* based on ten of his favorite Psalms, have been called "ten variations on the theme of God."[20] *Saint Ludmila,* Dvorak's dramatic oratorio, celebrates the conversion of the Czechs to Chris-tianity. During a pagan festival to a goddess, the hermit Ivan shatters her statue and calls upon all present to worship instead the one true God whose Son died upon the cross. He wins the young Princess and her future husband, Borivoj, to Christ, and the work culminates with their joyous baptism into the new faith.[21]

Dvorak created a great deal of sacred music,[22] yet many projects he dreamed of were never realized. He wanted to write oratorios entitled *Nazareth* and *Golgotha,*[23] but could never find suitable librettists.[24] Anyone attempting to compose a *Golgotha,* he concluded, needed an extra measure of self-assurance: he must "have such a head," Dvorak said, and he spread his hands wide.[25] At one point, Dvorak began writing sketches for a choral version of "The Song of Songs." But his conservative and old fashioned personality overruled, and he abandoned the work; the text seemed to him "too sensual."[26]

Dvorak attended the Bohemian Catholic Church, yet the faith he ex-pressed in his life and his music was nonsectarian. The same Dvorak who wrote a Latin *Requiem* also depicted his beliefs in his *Hussite Overture,* glorifying the ministry of Czech reformer John Hus.[27] His biographer Sourek concludes, "Dvorak's piety was a piety of the heart, of one who is devoted to God from conviction and not to some particular religious community. Dvorak was convinced to the depths of his being that over the world there watches a higher power which directs everything for the best: and he was devoted to that power with fervor and gratitude."[28]

His faith and his life mirrored one another; both were simple, unpretentious, and steadfast. Even at the height of his fame, Dvorak always kept close to nature and often expressed himself by relating to the world God made.[29] He took frequent breaks from his work to gaze at flocks of pigeons and to feed them. As a child, he was once asked to kneel for prayer. He responded, "I like praying best there at the window when I look out on the green and at the sky."[30] Dvorak's legacy as a great composer is enriched immeasurably by his consistent, childlike faith, untainted by a prosperous life of success and prestige.

SOME THOUGHTS ON DVORAK: ADAPTABILITY

The young Antonin Dvorak appeared to be thoroughly rustic; a humble, provincial man of the soil. Yet he would become a world traveler and international celebrity. Here was a man raised in poverty in the midst of men whose desperate need to put food on the table took captive any larger dreams or ambitions they might have harbored. Dvorak's own father, a struggling innkeeper, loved music and took pride in his son's talent, but opposed his training because it seemed presumptuous to imagine that a musician could keep from starving.

Yet Dvorak traveled around the globe, living in every conceivable setting. Within a decade of his first performances he was a world-famous composer, overwhelmed with commissions for new works. From his humble expectations, he had to adapt to a life of travel, public scrutiny and the company of thousands of adoring strangers. Of course, he never sought after cosmopolitan life; he would always be ill at ease in large cities and most comfortable in the company of a few good friends in a simple setting.

And the effect of all this acclaim on his personality? There was none. Although he readily accommodated great changes in lifestyle—from rural Bohemia to downtown New York City—he remained the same modest Anton that his friends had always known. Even after he achieved worldwide fame (which continued to amaze him), the renowned Dr. Dvorak still felt shy and uncomfortable around those he considered his social superiors.

Perhaps Dvorak could handle the stress of his flight to fame because he never lost the youthful innocence and vivacity of his childhood. He loved to play games with people of all ages. Even as an adult, he had a boyish passion for trains and ocean liners. He cherished children (especially his own), and had an outdoorsman's love of animals. Once, when two of his acquaintances were discussing Dvorak, one of them complained that all he knew was music. The other friend, better acquainted with the composer, countered, "Did you try talking to him about pigs?"

Ultimately, Dvorak's genuine disposition remained unaffected by changes in status because of the composer's profound love for mankind. Since he delighted more in a good friend than in the luxury of riches, he was able to be flexible in the most foreign surroundings. He was convinced that congenial people were to be found everywhere. From the commoners of Bohemia and Spillville, Iowa, to the sophisticates of London and New York, Dvorak remained the same. He adapted to every situation with good humor, and both his music and his character remained uncorrupted by his universal success.

RECOMMENDED LISTENING:

Orchestral Music: Nine Symphonies, notably Symphony No. 9, in E minor, ("From the New World"); Slavonic Dances; Carnival Overture; Concerti for Violin and Cello.

Chamber music: Quartet in F major, ("American"); Quintet in E-flat major; Trio in E minor, ("Dumky").

Piano Music: Humoresques.

Songs: Biblical Songs.

Choral Music: Requiem; Stabat Mater.

Opera: Saint Ludmila; Russalka.

"Most of the
forward
movements
of life
in general…
have been the
work of essential
religious-minded
men."

11

CHARLES
IVES
1874 - 1954

A passerby listening to the jarring song and accompaniment coming from the Connecticut house would never have believed a music lesson was in progress. More likely, the odd-sounding noise would be chalked up to the antics of pre-teen boys mocking a matronly piano teacher. Yet a lesson is exactly what is happening.

The father, an innovative bandmaster, sits at the piano methodically playing Stephen Foster's *Swannee River* in the key of C. His ten-year-old son struggles to keep up with the accompaniment as he sings the lyrics. The boy finds he is up against a difficult challenge: his father insists he sing in the key of E flat.

The young boy grimaces in concentration. Producing the correct vocal line to this accompaniment takes not only vocal control, but an advanced understanding of music theory. "Again!" cries the father. Finally, the father calls a halt to his outrageous venture. The boy's relief is profound, yet the clashing sounds linger in his memory and ignite a lifelong curiosity about breaching the boundaries of traditional music.

The boy's father, meanwhile, is delighted with his progress. He proclaims, "Now that kind of exercise will really help you to stretch your ears." Based on the compositions Charles Ives would eventually create, it seems these experimental lessons worked.

Charles Ives, a wonderful and notorious composer from the United States, appears to be several men rolled into one. The New Englander excelled in many areas, becoming a composer, a successful insurance executive, an excellent athlete, a political idealist, an Emersonian visionary, and a hymn-singing advocate for "that old time religion."[1] Even his friends had a hard time agreeing on who he was: their descriptions range from lauding Ives as a humble, shy, lover of mankind,[2] to censuring him as an opinionated, crotchety old man who could explode at a moment's notice.[3]

Ives was born in Danbury, Connecticut, on October 20, 1874. His father, George Ives, was a gifted musician but a very unconventional music teacher.[4] Later in life, when asked about his musical training, Charles Ives would simply reply, "Pa taught me what I know." He also remembered, "Father thought that a man as a rule did not use the facilities that the Creator had given hard enough."[5] So the bandmaster persisted in subjecting his talented son to a wide variety of experimental musical concepts. It is no surprise that the name Charles Ives eventually became synonymous with outlandish dissonance, polytonality (he said he liked to "hog all the keys"), and even the beginnings of what is now called aleatory or "chance" music.

Today there are Charles Ives Music Festivals; scholarly editions of his works; books, articles, and even a "Charles Ives Society." Yet this widely celebrated man remained virtually unknown until he stopped writing music about 1925.[6] He was quite shy about his compositions and never tried to force his music on the public. Often, years would go by before he heard his works performed, and many more years passed before their genius was understood and appreciated. His *Third Symphony* was not played until 35 years after it was written. When it finally emerged from obscurity, it won the Pulitzer Prize for Music.

Ives' music tested the limits of conventional composition and introduced many unexpected and novel elements. A typical work is his complex *Second String Quartet,* subtitled "String Quartet for four men—who converse, discuss, argue, fight, shake hands, shut up—then walk to the mountainside to view the firmament." In another work, entitled *All the Way Around and Back,* Ives included this handwritten notation: "foul ball—and the base runner on 3rd has to go all the way back to 1st."

As a young man, Ives enrolled in Yale to study music, but he dumbfounded his teachers, maintaining a consistent D+ average. This was primarily because he spent so much time excelling at baseball, football and track. One of his coaches declared it a "crying shame" that such a natural athlete wasted so much time in music.[7]

After graduating, Ives abandoned music as a career, believing his unconventional compositions would never attract the popular following needed to make a living. Instead, he entered the insurance business, insisting that he did not want his family to "starve on my dissonances." He eventually co-founded a flourishing insurance company, known as Ives and Myrick. In this field he was also a pioneer, developing the first training course for representatives and formulating the concept of estate planning. The firm prospered and became one of the largest of its kind in the country.[8]

At night and on weekends, Ives shed his businessman's demeanor and immersed himself in composing. Late into the night he experimented on the piano, creating vast quantities of his ultra-complex music. His neighbors frequently objected to the din, complaining that he created "resident disturbances."[9]

Ives' faith and his musical genius are inseparable. Even as a boy, he played the organ for many different churches,[10] giving him a life-long affinity for sacred choral music.[11] He set to music numerous psalms,[12] and he borrowed extensively from gospel hymn tunes, often highlighting them in the most unusual musical circumstances. From his orchestral compositions to his multifarious chamber music, more than fifty different hymn tunes are "quoted,"[13] such as *Jesus, Lover of My Soul, Just As I Am Without One Plea*, and *What a Friend We Have in Jesus*.[14] His complete works contain dozens of religious titles and references, from *The Revival Service* to *General William Booth Enters Into Heaven*.[15]

Ives frequented the outdoor revivals of his time, and their rugged, homespun music affected him deeply.[16] He perceived an authentic, if roughhewn, faith at work among the people who turned out to hear itinerant preachers and evangelists. In his typical, rugged manner, Ives considered these revivals, "a man's experience for men."[17] And hearing them sing brought Ives in touch with the raw persuasion of music. "There was power and exaltation in these great concaves of sound",[18] he wrote, "sung by thousands of 'let out' souls", as he called them.[19] Sometimes he accompanied the singing himself on the melodeon (a small reed organ),[20] and he listened closely, intrigued, as the fervor of the singing would often throw the key as much as a whole tone higher. His father, who usually led the outdoor congregations with his cornet,[21] had a special sliding valve added so he could rise with the singers and not keep them down![22]

Ives brought the same sort of eclectic mix of influences to his religious faith as he applied to his music, and perhaps that is why his strong faith has been largely misunderstood. It is a curious combination of seemingly opposing forces: on one hand, it is rooted in the "uncivilized" Holy Ghost revivals and open-air preaching he loved[23] and which many secular biographers fail to understand or appreciate. On the other hand, Ives found personal inspiration in the writings of the great American transcendentalists, notably Emerson and Thoreau.[24] These meditations, in turn, are rarely understood or appreciated by revivalists and fundamentalist Christians.

But Ives saw no contradiction. He lived simultaneously in both worlds and developed a truly unique Christian faith: a childlike yet masculine trust in God, inseparably linked with intellectual integrity. If the transcendentalists and "the prayer-meeting evangelists disagreed on doctrine," wrote one of Ives' biographers, "it seems neither to have upset him or even to have occurred to him."[25]

People close to the composer knew him as deeply religious[26] and very strict on matters of morality.[27] Ives did not bow to intellectual pressure to disparage religious faith. He observed, "Most of the forward movements of life in general and of pioneers in most of the great activities, have been the work of essential religious-minded men."[28] He openly looked forward to life after death, noting that he wanted to "see and talk to my father."[29]

Ives enjoyed a long and happy marriage to Harmony Twichell, a daughter of a prominent Hartford minister. She was known as a devout woman, who regularly read the Bible aloud to her husband.[30] Despite his Protestant background, Ives maintained an open-minded outlook on the different views of various denominations.[31] Robert M. Crunden, who lectured on the composer's beliefs at the Charles Ives Centennial Festival in 1974, said, "Ives's religion was definitely Christian, but he had no illusions about the stuffiness of churches on many occasions."[32] Ives once observed that "every thinking man knows that the church part of the church always has been dead—that part seen by candle-light, not Christ-light."[33]

Many present-day devotees of Ives' music tend to emphasize the transcendental influence present in his life and work. Perhaps this is a reflection of their own sense of distance from "hell-fire evangelists" and emotional revival meetings. But his principle biographer, John Kirkpatrick, who knew Ives better than anyone living today, wrote: "His church-going self was conservative to the point of fundamentalism. He was almost in a state of 'Give me that old time religion, it's good enough for me.'"[34]

Some Thoughts on Ives: Unselfishness

In an era when composers often stand accused of lusting after fame, money, or both, it is refreshing to discover a man such as Charles Ives. He knew that both fame and wealth were within his grasp, and he chose neither. Perhaps he saw the folly of chasing such fantasies, or perhaps he simply had better things to do.

Ives' prosperous insurance company could have made him a millionaire many times over, but he insisted on being paid only what would befit his family's needs. He also refused to accept money derived from his musical genius. When he won the coveted Pulitzer Prize in 1947, he told the award committee, "Prizes are for boys. I'm grown up." Ives gave away the $500 prize money.

At first, he actually objected to copyrighting his compositions, firmly believing that everyone should have free access to his work. Finally he did submit to the usual copyright procedures, but only on the condition that any profits his music earned would go toward aiding the publication of young composers. His personal generosity toward fellow musicians is legendary.

As to fame, Ives all but hid from it. In his later years, when he began to be proclaimed a genius, he became conspicuously absent from performances of his own work. The composer's nephew, who knew him well, remembers an approachable, unpretentious man: "I never had any compunction about violating the privacy of Uncle Charlie's music studio. In fact, Uncle Charlie never called it a studio. That would have been too fancy a term. It was just a room where the piano was."

This simplicity did not arise out of insecurity or self-doubt. On the contrary, he privately made it clear that he thought his compositions were greater than Mozart's: "I state that it *is* better! Ask any good musician—those who don't agree with me are not good musicians." But he steadfastly refused to be taken in by worldly trappings. His secretary once asked Ives for an autograph to give her son, and he replied, "The only time you get my autograph is on a check."

Ives reserved a particular fondness for everyday people. "He was always interested in the underprivileged and physically handicapped," his nephew recalled. "He had a sincere interest in anyone who needed help." Although he could explode with rage over such issues as war and politics, he extended kindness to the humblest acquaintance. A widow who worked as the Ives' housekeeper for 17 years cherishes distinct memories of the famous composer:

Ives regularly made friendly jokes, insisted on helping with the dishes, and played hymns on the piano, she recalled.

Such unguarded moments of the man round out a portrait of Charles Ives. He was not just the revolutionary innovator, but also a generous, down-to-earth man who loved God and people. His fame was late in coming, but his ultimate influence on other composers has been extraordinary. His famous fellow-composer Igor Stravinsky concluded, "Ives was an original man, a gifted man, a courageous man. Let us honor him through his works."

RECOMMENDED LISTENING:

Orchestral Music: Four Symphonies, Lincoln, the Great Commoner, The Unanswered Question, Robert Browning Overture.

Chamber Music: Two String Quartets.

Vocal Music: General William Booth Enters Into Heaven, Psalm 24, 54, 67, 90.

Piano Music: Second Piano Sonata ("Concord, Mass., 1840-60").

"The more one separates oneself from the canons of the Christian church, the further one distances oneself from the truth."

12

IGOR
STRAVINSKY

1882 - 1971

It is 1913, and a ballet performance in Paris is agitating its audience into extreme pandemonium. Greeting the ballet's first notes from a solo bassoon are rancorous catcalls from parts of the audience. Others bellow back, defending the peculiar music and dance on the stage. Soon the orchestra is all but drowned out by the riotous din, but still the musicians and dancers persevere.

The music's rhythmic power so overcomes one man in the audience that he begins beating his fists upon the head of the man sitting in front of him. In the aisles, tuxedo-clad Frenchmen punch each other like ruffians. The Austrian Ambassador laughs aloud in scorn; a princess storms out of the theatre, fuming that she's been made a fool of; and a duel is arranged between two strangers who disagree about the music.

Famous musicians in the audience react with similar passions. In the middle of the maelstrom, Saint-Saens is heard repeating over and over "He is crazy, he is crazy!" Capu screams that the music is a huge fraud, but Ravel shouts "Genius!" Roland-Manuel boldly defends the music and gets his collar torn from his shirt, while Debussy pleads futilely with everyone to quiet down so he can hear. Backstage, trying valiantly to hold back more fights, stands the diminutive composer. The premiere of his *Rite of Spring* becomes a turning point in western art, and Igor Stravinsky emerges as the musical master of his century.

There was practically no genre of music beyond the command of Igor Stravinsky, widely considered the most important composer of the twentieth century. He wrote ballet and chamber music, opera, choral, and orchestral music, and that's not all. He composed a polka for Ringling Brothers/Barnum & Bailey Circus and a clarinet concerto for Benny Goodman.

Born in a suburb of St. Petersburg, Russia, Stravinsky received scant encouragement to follow in the musical footsteps of his father, a successful opera singer. Like several composers before him, Stravinsky found himself steered firmly toward the study of law—a more stable and secure way to make a living, so his father believed. Stravinsky obliged his parents, but he continued to compose music whenever he could. Eventually, his devotion to music prevailed and he abandoned his legal studies.

In his early twenties, Stravinsky became the private student of Russian composer Rimsky-Korsakoff. Soon, his genius came to be recognized by the musical world. He gained international attention with the premieres of three great ballets, commissioned by Diaghilev, the renowned director of the Russian Ballet. These works, *Firebird, Petrushka,* and the indomitable *Rite of Spring,* subtitled "Pictures of Pagan Russia" remain in the repertoire of every major orchestra in the world today.

Stravinsky's early ballets explore secular and even pagan subjects that offer no clue as to the personal religious faith he possessed later in life. These great works were written when Stravinsky was in his thirties and had long since abandoned the Russian Orthodox faith of his upbringing.[1] Yet in the mid 1920s, Stravinsky experienced a permanent conversion to Christianity.[2]

In the church of his childhood, Stravinsky had been required to read the Bible.[3] He began criticizing and rebelling against the Church when he reached his teens,[4] and he parted ways with Orthodoxy for nearly three decades. Yet late in life he would explain, "For some years before my conversion, a mood of acceptance had been cultivated in me by a reading of the Gospels and by other religious literature."[5]

Two incidents appeared to assure his new-found faith in Christ. One was an immediate and convincing answer to a private prayer,[6] and the other was a healing experience. Stravinsky developed a painful abscess on his right forefinger, and its insistent throbbing threatened to keep him from performing his *Piano Sonata.* He prayed about the problem but fully expected the concert would have to be canceled.

The pain hounded him all the way to the stage. Later he explained to his friend Robert Craft: "My finger was still festering when I walked onto the stage at the Teatro La Fevice, and I addressed the audience, apologizing in advance for what would have to be a poor performance. I sat down, removed the little bandage, felt the pain had suddenly stopped, and discovered that the finger was—miraculously, it seemed to me—healed."[7]

Soon, Stravinsky began to speak openly of his convictions. In an interview in Brussels, the composer stated, "The more one separates oneself from the canons of the Christian church, the further one distances oneself from the truth.... Art is made of itself, and one cannot create upon a creation, even though we are ourselves graftings of Jesus Christ."[8]

He dedicated his next major composition, the *Symphony of Psalms,* to the glory of God.[9] Like so many of the biblical passages this work contains, the *Symphony of Psalms* expresses an awakening sense of distance from the Creator, and the human choice to return to the Creator. "The first movement was written in a state of religious and musical ebullience," Stravinsky explained. The second movement, Psalm 40, "is a prayer that the new canticle may be put into our mouths. The Alleluia [third movement] is that canticle."[10]

Francis Routh, one of Stravinsky's biographers, insisted, "No composer could write such a work without a very secure, rock-like, religious faith."[11] Another biographer, Alexandre Tansman, wrote, "He is a believer in the full sense of the term."[12] Stravinsky's colleague and principle biographer Robert Craft agrees. He has written, "Having lived for more than a quarter of a century with Stravinsky, and much of that under the same roof, I knew him to be, as the saying goes, profoundly religious."[13]

The composer had strong opinions about the purpose and use of music. "The church knew what the Psalmist knew: music praises God. Music is as well or better able to praise Him than the building of the church and all its decorations; it is the church's greatest ornament."[14] When asked if one must be a believer to compose church music, Stravinsky asserted, "Certainly, and not merely a believer in 'symbolic figures,' but in the person of the Lord, the person of the Devil, and the miracles of the church."[15]

Stravinsky had his quirks, and some of them found expression in the way he integrated faith into his life. He grumbled about the "you who's" in new translations of the Bible,[16] and he always prayed in the Slavonic language of the Russian liturgy.[17] Other eccentricities were innocuous and endearing. Stravinsky often balanced an extra pair of glasses on top of his head in case he lost the pair he was wearing!

Once his biographer Craft accompanied the composer to his Orthodox Church. As soon as he entered, Stravinsky prostrated himself flat on the floor before the altar and prayed. For two hours, the two men knelt on a hard, uncushioned floor. After taking the sacraments, Stravinsky again prayed with his head touching the floor.[18]

The composer certainly loved his church, yet he retained a sense of honest detachment from it. He wrote *Three Sacred Choruses* to be used in its liturgy,[19] stating that the work was "inspired by the bad music and worse singing in the Russian Church."[20] Harboring no sectarian prejudice, he also wrote a Catholic Mass which, he believed, "appeals directly to the spirit."[21] Other works based on sacred texts include *The Flood, The Tower of Babel, Abraham and Isaac, Requiem Canticles, Sermon, a Narrative and a Prayer, Threni, Canticum Sacrum,* a *Credo,* an *Ave Maria,* and a *Pater Noster.*

In his work, Stravinsky found expression for his views on Christianity. In his working notes to *The Flood,* for instance, he described Noah "as an *Old Testament* Christ-figure, like Melchizedek."[22] He seemed especially preoccupied with the nature of evil, writing, "As Satan's falsetto aria with flutes is a prolepsis of Christianity, Satan must now be shown as Anti-Christ."[23] He went on to make a thought-provoking theological observation, noting that Lucifer is "inclined to take his position for granted, which is why true Christians can overcome him."[24]

Throughout his life Stravinsky was known for his integrity and candor. Concerning his genius, he wrote, "I regard my talents as God-given, and I have always prayed to Him for strength to use them. When in early childhood I discovered that I had been made the custodian of musical aptitudes, I pledged myself to God to be worthy of their development, though, of course, I have broken the pledge and received uncovenanted mercies all my life, and though the custodian has all too often kept faith on his all-too-worldly terms."[25]

Stravinsky faced up to his own imperfections without flinching. In his personal writings entitled "Thoughts of an Octogenarian," he observed, "I was born out of time in the sense that by temperament and talent I would have been more suited for the life of a small Bach, living in anonymity and composing regularly for an established service and for God. I did weather the world I was born to, weathered it well you will say, and I have survived—though not uncorrupted."[26]

Once he replied to what he considered an unfair criticism of the vocal writing of his sacred music, commenting dryly, "One hopes to worship God with a little art if one has any, and if one hasn't, and cannot recognize it in others, then one can at least burn a little incense."[27] Concerning the origin of his innovative compositions, he was almost blunt in his modesty: "Only God can create. I make music from music."[28]

Stravinsky lived a full, long life enriched by a wide circle of friends, all of whom respected his Christian beliefs. As he concluded in his acclaimed "Poetics of Music," he believed "Music comes to reveal itself as a form of communion with our fellow man—and with the Supreme Being."[29]

SOME THOUGHTS ON STRAVINSKY: INTEGRITY

Stravinsky's many years as a composer were lived in the public eye. His life and his work have endured more scrutiny than any serious composer of this century. Yet the more one studies this man, the more he appears as a Gibraltar who remained unshaken by the opinions and pressures of the world around him. To maintain his personal integrity, he spent decades "going against the grain." He managed to preserve a basic consistency which was rarely seen in the lives of his artistic colleagues.

To begin with, Stravinsky was a musical pathfinder, establishing bold new concepts yet remaining unruffled by the often venomous criticism his innovations provoked. He was not an imitator; he followed his own lead, single-handedly creating whole schools of musical thought. After stretching the bounds of complexity in his early ballets, he championed neo-classicism, and later even tried his hand at serial compositions. Yet none of these moves came about because of exterior pressures or intimidation. Stravinsky leaves the impression that if he ever used a device that was common among other composers, it was due to coincidence rather than imitation.

His spiritual life reflected his moral integrity. When he later came to believe the truth of Christianity, Stravinsky did not hesitate to declare himself openly a convert. He even wrote his famous collaborator, Diaghilev, to explain his new convictions and ask forgiveness for any wrong he may have ever committed against him. He seemed to consider honest acknowledgement to be the only consistent choice before him. His religious beliefs, which might have drawn ridicule from the world, were repeatedly asserted without hesitation or apology.

After his conversion, Stravinsky led a consistent spiritual life which adhered without compromise to its standards. Many first-hand evidences of his religious congruity are told with respect by colleagues who did not share his faith. In their presence, the composer worshiped unblushingly, showed displeasure or even irritation at things he considered blasphemous, and spoke openly about his Christian faith and its effect on his life and work.

Stravinsky held deep convictions and he could be adamant about them. This was not due to a quarrelsome spirit, but rather to his unconquerable integrity. Yet with all the controversy his music created, he still welcomed an encouraging word. When a friend informed Stravinsky that he was preparing a biography about him, the composer answered, "If you are really writing a book about me, say what you have to say." Then he added with a smile, "But please be kind."

RECOMMENDED LISTENING:

Orchestral Music: Suites from The Fire-Bird, Petrouchka, The Rite of Spring, Symphonies of Wind Instruments; Symphony in C major, Concerto for Violin.

Chamber Music: The Soldier's Tale; Octet for Winds.

Piano Music: Sonata for Piano.

Choral Music: Symphony of Psalms, Pater Noster, Mass.

Opera: The Nightingale; The Flood.

Afterword

The study of great composers' lives should be more than academic exercise. Biography is to inspire, not merely inform. This being the case, a question remains: What does it mean to us that these composers shared a common faith in God?

In part, the answer must be a personal one. To me, it is a great encouragement to learn about the faith of noted composers who lived years before me. As I researched this work, I felt challenged by Ives' unselfishness and Beethoven's determination. Similarly, seeking to unravel the mysteries of Liszt's faith and Wagner's jumbled belief system deepened my understanding of how Christian faith relates to everyday life.

Beyond my own personal journey of discovery about these composers, however, I believe there are other compelling reasons for learning about their faith. To begin with, after studying not only these twelve men, but also the lives of dozens of other great composers, I have discovered an unmistakably high degree of belief. The composers selected for this book were certainly not the only masters with spiritual convictions—far from it. It could have contained Vivaldi, Bruckner, Franck, Corelli, Vaughan Williams, Messaien, or many others. There are, of course, some exceptions, but not as many as you might think.

What I conclude, based on a large amount of biographical evidence, is that the composers are, as a group, surprisingly and often deeply religious. Even those with the most secular lifestyles always seem to have a sincere respect for the Deity—a hunger for something greater than themselves which transcends everyday existence.

Why is this the case? Is it an extra sensitivity? Does it arise out of an almost god-like compulsion within a composer to create something that previously did not exist? I am reminded of something once said by Albert Einstein, a genius from another field of creativity: "The more I study physics, the more I'm drawn to metaphysics." Perhaps composers and creative geniuses detect spiritual realities to which others are generally unaware.

The sensitivity of these masters led them to a common conclusion, summarized by Beethoven: "It was not a fortuitous meeting of chordal atoms that made the world; if order and beauty are reflected in the constitution of the universe, then there is a God." These composers, who always realize that their most appreciative audiences will appear long after their death, were seldom satisfied with the superficiality and materialism of this life.

Their faith throughout the ages cannot help but suggest that Christian experience is authentic, that it is based on verifiable evidence, and that it finds expression in a wide variety of ways.

Remember the words of Stravinsky, when asked about his conversion to Christianity in his forties? The composer did not mention the actions of theologians or denominations, he said he was convinced by "a reading of the Gospels". He went directly to the source—to Jesus' original teachings: that God loves all men, that mankind is fallen and in need of redemption, that Jesus Christ died on a cross to pay the penalty for man's sins, and that we must believe in Christ and his sacrifice for us to obtain salvation. It was here that the composer found the truth upon which he could base his life.

All too often we tend to associate, and even equate religion with this-or-that church, movement, or denomination. Yet Bach himself, perhaps the most conventional churchman of this book, believed quite a mix of doctrines that no single church contained. The basis for these composers' beliefs was not an external structure, but an internal, personal relationship between each of them and Christ. Their faith grew, not by mere acquiescence to what they were taught by their parents or their priests, but by deep soul-searching, groping, and determination to discern the truth for themselves.

The very diversity of authentic Christian belief displayed by these composers also challenges me not to condemn other Christians who do not believe precisely as I do. It is so easy to fall into the error of judging those who attend different churches, adhere to different denominations, or even worship in different styles. Not only did these twelve composers come from a wide variety of denominations, but each of them respected Christians from dissimilar backgrounds.

Finally, a point might be made against criticisms and our twentieth century viewpoint of the faults of these very human composers. Once, after lecturing on Mozart's faith, a fellow Christian remonstrated with me over the small set of letters that the composer wrote as a youth which are rife with profanity.

Rather than trying to defend Mozart for what was obviously profane, I found myself asking, "Would you want everything you've ever written or said to be published and studied by posterity?"

It never hurts to be reminded that *our* "biographers" are indeed all around us—they are the ones who observe our daily lives, feel the influence of our words, actions and emotions. The fact of our intense interest in the lives of composers who lived centuries before us provides a sobering reminder: Do *we* live with integrity, lives that are consistent with our beliefs?

After spending years scrutinizing these composers' lives to find what they believed, I am left with the serious question for myself, and for all of us: "If a biographer should someday research my life, what tangible verifications of my faith would be evident?" Perhaps the greatest lesson we can learn from these musicians, both in failure and success, involves the value of self-examination in light of what we understand about God.

These composers experienced a personal faith in a loving God, who gave their lives purpose. They recognized that their musical talents were a gift from God, and they determined to use these gifts to the utmost. As we have seen, they were not men without problems; and in some cases their troubles were at least partly self-imposed. But their faith in God enabled them to prevail despite their difficulties, and to create masterpieces that have enriched the lives of many generations. Understanding their faith augments our appreciation of their music and their individuality, and it brings us back again to a personal response.

The experience of Christianity is meant for all times. A common thread of faith links each of these composers whose lives span three centuries. Fortunately, their spiritual experiences continue to be available to us today. Their faith has inspired my faith, and I hope it has inspired yours as well.

NOTES

NOTES FOR CHAPTER 1 - GEORGE FRIDERIC HANDEL

1   Richard D. Dinwiddie, "Messiah, Behind the Scenes of Handel's Masterpiece", Christianity Today (Dec. 17, 1982), p. 16.

2   John Allanson Benson, *Handel's Messiah, the Oratorio and its History* (London: Reeves, 1897), p. 2.

3   Watkins Shaw, *A Textual and Historical Companion to Handel's Messiah* (Borough Green: Novello, Ltd., 1965), p. 24.

4   Newman Flower, *Handel, His Personality and His Times* (London: Panther Books, Ltd., 1919), p. 272.

5   Ibid., p. 272.

6   Myers, *Handel's Messiah, A Touchstone of Taste* (New York: Octagon Books, 1971), p. 63.

7   Hertha Pauli, *Handel and the Messiah Story* (New York: Meredith, 1968), p. 51.

8   Charles Hazilip Webb, *Handel's Messiah: A Conductor's View* (Bloomington: Indiana University Press, 1978), p. 4.

9   Robert Manson Myers, *Early Criticism of Handelian Oratorio* (Williamsburg: Manson Park Press, 1947), p. 18.

10 John Mainwaring, *Memoirs of the Life of George Frideric Handel* (London: Dodsley, 1860), p. 136.

11 A. E. Bray, *Handel, His Life, Personal and Professional* (London: Ward & Company, 1857),p. 63.

12 Percy M. Young, *The Oratorios of Handel* (London: Dobson, Ltd., 1949), p. 100.

13 Myers, *Handel's Messiah, A Touchstone of Taste*, op. cit., p. 238.

14 John Tobin, *Handel's Messiah, A Critical Account of the Manuscript Sources and Printed Editions* (New York: St. Martins Press, Inc., 1969), p. 161.

15 William Coxe, *Anecdotes of George Frideric Handel and John Christopher Smith* (London: Bulmer, 1799), p. 29.

16 Myers, *Handel's Messiah, A Touchstone of Taste*, op. cit., p. 80.

17 Winton Dean, *Handel* (New York: W. W. Norton & Company, 1980), p. 74.

18 Myers, *Handel's Messiah, A Touchstone of Taste*, op. cit., pp. 79-80.

19 Erich H. Muller, *The Letters and Writings of George Frideric Handel* (Freeport: Books for Libraries Press, 1970), p. 86.

20 Paul Henry Lang, *George Frideric Handel* (New York: W. W. Norton & Company, 1966), p. 104.

21 Tobin, op. cit., p. 161.

22 Robert Turnbull, *Musical Genius and Religion* (London: S. Wellwood Publishers, 1907), p. 27.

23 Otto Erich Deutsch, *Handel, A Documentary Biography* (London: Adam & Charles Black, 1955), p. 819.

24 Flower, op. cit., p. 333.

25 Dinwiddie, op. cit., p. 19.

OTHER SOURCES:

Cummings, William Hayman. *Handel*. London: G. Bell & Sons, 1904.

Larsen, Jens P. *Handel's Messiah*. New York: W. W. Norton, 1972.

Rockstro, William Smith. *The Life of George Frederick Handel*. London: Macmillan & Company, 1883.

Schoelcher, Victor. *The Life of Handel*. London: Trubner & Company, 1857.

Smith, William Charles. *Concerning Handel: His Life and Works*. London: Cassell & Company, 1948.

Smith, William Charles. *George III, Handel and Mainwaring.* Musical Times, lxv, 1924, p. 789.
Smith, William Charles. "Handeliana". Music and Letters, xxxi, 1950, p. 125; xxxiv, 1953, p. 11.
Streatfeild, Richard Alexander. *Handel.* London: Methuen Publishers, 1909.
Townsend, Horath. *An Account of the Visit of Handel to Dublin with Incidental Notices of His Life and Character.* Dublin: J. McGlashan Publishers, 1852.
Young, Percy Marshall. *Handel.* London: J. M. Dent Company, 1975.

NOTES FOR CHAPTER 2 - JOHANN SEBASTIAN BACH

1   Johann Nikolaus Forkel, *Johann Sebastian Bach, His Life, His Art, and Work* (New York: Da Capo Press, 1970), p. 106.
2   Sedley Taylor, *Life of J.S. Bach: Church Musician and Composer* (Cambridge: MacMillan & Bowes, 1897), p. 52.
3   Robert W. S. Mendl, *The Divine Quest in Music* (New York: Philosophical Library, 1957), p. 59.
4   Friedrich Blume, *Two Centuries of Bach, An Account of Changing Tastes* (London: Oxford University Press, 1950), p. 14.
5   Max Hinrichen, *Hinrichen's Musical Year Book (Vol. VII)* (London: Hinrichen Editions Ltd., 1952), p. 263.
6   Albert Schweitzer, *J. S. Bach* (New York: Dover Publications, 1911), p. 166-7.
7   Paul Hindemith, *Johann Sebastian Bach, Heritage and Obligation* (New Haven: Yale University Press, 1952), p. 35.
8   Charles Hubert Hasting Perry, *J.S. Bach - The Story of the Development of a Great Personality* (Westport, CT: Greenwood Press, 1970), p. 533.
9   Hans Theodore David and Arthur Mendel, *The Bach Reader* (New York: W. W. Norton & Company, 1966), p. 24.
10 Ibid., pp. 60, 67, 92, 111, 115, 125, 128, 151 and, 160.
11 Karl Geiringer, *Johann Sebastian Bach, Culmination of an Era* (New York: Oxford University Press, 1966), p. 87.
12 Wilibald Gurlitt, *Johann Sebastian Bach, the Master and His Work* (St. Louis: Concordia Publishing House, 1957), p. 12.
13 David and Mendel, op. cit., p. 98.
14 Charles Sanford Terry, *The Music of Bach, An Introduction* (New York: Dover Publications, 1963), p. 17.
15 Gerhard Herz, "Bach's Religion", Journal of Renaissance and Baroque Music, Vol. 1, #2 (June 1946), p.126.
16 Wilfrid Mellers, *Bach and the Dance of God* (New York: Da Capo Press, 1981), p. 155.
17 Herz, op. cit., pp.132-133.
18 Robin Leaver, *J. S. Bach as Preacher* (St. Louis: Concordia Publishing House, 1982), p. 13.
19 Ibid., p. 13.
20 Ibid., p. 13.
21 Leo Schrade, "Bach: The Conflict Between the Sacred and the Secular", Journal of the History of Ideas, Vol.VII #2 (New York, College of the City of New York, April 1946), p. 166.
22 Paul Frederick Foelber, *Bach's Treatment of the Subject of Death in his Choral Music* (St. Louis: Concordia Publishing House, 1961), p. 7.
23 Herz, op. cit., p.135.
24 Paul Sauer, *The Life-Work of J.S. Bach* (St. Louis: Concordia Publishing House, 1929), p. 6.
25 Philipp Spitta, *Johann Sebastian Bach* (New York: Dover Publications, 1951), pp. 275.

OTHER SOURCES:

Buhrman, Thomas Scott Godfrey. *Bach's Life: Chronologically as He Lived It.* New York: Organ Interests, Inc., 1935.
Cox, Howard H. *The Calov Bible of Bach.* Ann Arbor: UMI Research Press, 1985.
Dickinson, Allen Edgar Frederic. *The Art of J. S. Bach.* London: Duckworth Publishers, 1935.

Field, Lawrence. *Johann Sebastian Bach.* Minneapolis: Augsburg Publishing, 1943.

Geiringer, Karl. *The Bach Family: Seven Generations of Creative Genius.* New York: Oxford University Press, 1954.

Grew, Eva and Sidney. *Bach.* New York: McGraw-Hill Book Company, 1947.

Miles, Russell Hancock. *Johann Sebastian Bach.* Englewood Cliffs, New Jersey: Prentice Hall, 1962.

Millar, Cynthia. *Bach and His World.* Norristown: Silver Brunett, 1980.

Newman, Werner. *Bach, A Pictorial Biography.* London: Thames & Hudson, 1961.

Rimbault, E. F. *J.S. Bach, His Life and Writings.* London: Metzler & Co., 1869.

Terry, Charles Sanford. *Bach: A Biography.* London: Oxford University Press, 1928.

Terry, Charles Sanford. *Bach, Cantatas, Oratorio, Passion, Magnificat, and Motets.* New York: Oxford University Press, 1923.

Thorne, Edward Henry. *Bach.* London: G. Bell & Sons, 1904.

Young, Percy Marshall. *The Bachs: 1500-1850.* London: Boosey & Hawks, 1970.

NOTES FOR CHAPTER 3 - FRANZ JOSEPH HAYDN

1 Rosemary Hughes, *Haydn* (London: J.M. Dent & Sons LTD, 1966), p. 4.
2 Ibid., p. 5.
3 Ibid., p. 18.
4 George August Griesinger, *Biographical Notes Concerning Joseph Haydn* (Madison: University of Wisconsin Press, 1963), p. 56.
5 Hughes, op. cit., p. 47.
6 Christina Stadtlaender, *Joseph Haydn of Eisenstadt* (London: Dennis Dobson, 1968), p. 66.
7 Albert Christoph Dies, *Biographical Accounts of Joseph Haydn* (Madison, University of Wisconsin Press, 1963), p. 139.
8 Heinrich Edward Jacob, *Joseph Haydn, his Art, Times and Glory* (Westport, CT: Greenwood Press, 1950), p. 273.
9 Brian Redfern, *Haydn, A Biography* (Hamden, CT: Archon Books, 1970), p. 35.
10 Jacob, op. cit., p. 272.
11 Ibid., pp. 272-273.
12 Ludwig Nohl, *The Life of Haydn* (St. Clair Shores, MI: Scholarly Press, 1970), p. 168.
13 Marion M. Scott, "Haydn: Relics and Reminiscences in England", Music and Letters, Vol. XIII, No. 2, (April 1932), p. 136.
14 Griesinger, op. cit., p. 54.
15 Henri Beyle, *Haydn, Mozart, and Metastasio* (New York: Grossman Publications, 1972), p. 149.
16 Griesinger, op. cit., pp. 53-54.
17 Howard Chandler Robbins Landon, *The Collected Correspondence and London Notebooks of Joseph Haydn* (Fairlawn, NJ: Essential Books, 1959), p. 187.
18 Neil Butterworth, *Haydn, His Life and Times* (Kent: Midas Books, 1977), p. 122.
19 Beyle, op. cit., pp. 149-150.
20 Scott, op. cit., p. 135-6.
21 Howard Chandler Robbins Landon, *Haydn, Chronicle and Works* (Bloomington: Indiana University Press, 1977), p. 439.
22 Walter Pass, "Melodic Construction in Haydn's Two Salve Regina Settings", from Haydn Studies; Proceedings of the International Haydn Conference, 1975, (New York: W. W. Norton & Co., 1981), p. 273.
23 Hurwitz, Joachim, "Haydn and the Freemasons", The Haydn Yearbook, Vol. XVI (1985), Bryn Mawr: Theodore Presser Company, p. 5.
24 Karl and Irene Geiringer, *Haydn, A Creative Life in Music* (Berkeley: University of California Press, 1968), p. 93.
25 Hughes, op. cit., p. 193.
26 Geiringer, op. cit., pp. 12-13.

27 Weiss Piero, *Letters of Composers through Seven Centuries* (Philadelphia: Chilton Book Company, 1976), p. 115.
28 Michel Brenet, *Haydn* (New York: Benjamin Blom, Inc., 1972), pp. 58-59.
29 James Cuthbert Hadden, *Haydn* (New York: AMS Press, 1977), p. 147.
30 Griesinger, op. cit., p. 54.
31 Herbert F. Peyser, *Joseph Haydn, Servant and Master* (New York: The Philharmonic Symphony Society of New York, 1950), p. 50.

OTHER SOURCES:

Gotwals, Vernon. "Joseph Haydn's Last Will and Testament". Musical Quarterly, 1961, p. 331.
Hadow, William Henry. *A Creation Composer.* Freeport, New York: Books for Libraries Press, 1972.
Hocker, Gustav. *Joseph Haydn.* Chicago: A. C. McClurg & Company, 1907.
Hollis, Helen R. *The Musical Instruments of Haydn.* Washington, D.C: Smithsonian Institution Press, 1977.
Lowens, Irving. *Haydn in America.* Detroit: College Music Society, 1979.
Olleson, Edward, "The Origin and Libbretto of Haydn's *Creation*", The Haydn Yearbook, Vol. IV (1968), Bryn Mawr: Theodore Presser Company.
Pohl, Karl Ferdinand. *Mozart and Haydn in London.* New York: Da Capo Press, 1970.
Runciman, John F. *Haydn.* London: G. Bell and Sons, 1908.
Young, Percy Marshall. *Haydn.* New York: D. White Company, 1969.

NOTES FOR CHAPTER 4 - WOLFGANG AMADEUS MOZART

1 Arthur Hutchings, *Mozart, the Man, the Musician* (London: Thames & Hudson, 1976) p. 101.
2 Friedrich Kerst, editor, *Mozart, the Man and the Artist Revealed in His own Words* (translated by Henry Krehbiel) (New York: Dover Publications, 1965) p. 95.
3 Alfred Einstein, *Mozart, His Character, His Work* (London: Cassell & Co. Ltd., 1946) p. 78.
4 Kerst., op. cit., p. 93.
5 Ibid., p. 96.
6 Ibid., p. 96.
7 Ludwig Nohl, *Life of Mozart* (London: Longmans, Green, and Co., 1877), pp. 59-60.
8 Einstein, op. cit., p. 79.
9 Otto Erich Deutsch, *Mozart; A Documentary Biography* (Stanford: Stanford University Press, 1965), p. 540.
10 Otto Jahn, *Life of Mozart* (New York: Cooper Square Publications, 1910) p. 267.
11 Paul Nettl, *Mozart and Masonry* (New York: Da Capo Press, 1957) p. 31.
12 Katherine Thomson, *The Masonic Thread in Mozart* (London: Lawrence & Wishart, 1977) p. 172.
13 Einstein, op cit., p. 85.
14 Hans Mersmann, editor, *Letters of Wolfgang Amadeus Mozart* (New York: Dover Publications, 1972) p. 111.
15 Kerst, op. cit., p. 96.
16 Ibid., p. 96.
17 Ibid., p. 95.
18 Ibid., p. 97.
19 Ibid., p. 97.
20 Walter James Turner, *Mozart, the Man and his Work* (Westport, Connecticut: Greenwood Press, 1938) p. 341.
21 Jahn, op. cit., pp. 391-392.
22 Ibid., p. 391.
23 Franz Nemetschek, *The Mozart Handbook,* edited by Louis Bianciolli (Westport, Connecticut: Greenwood Press, 1954) p. 146.
24 Michael Levey, *The Life and Death of Mozart* (London: Cardinal Publishers, 1971) p. 268.
25 Emily Anderson, editor, *The Letters of Mozart and his Family* (New York: St. Martins Press, 1966), p. 557.

Other Sources:

Blom, Eric. *Mozart.* London: Dent Publishers, 1975.

Blume, Friedrich. "Requiem But No Peace", The Musical Quarterly, New York: April, 1961, p. 147.

Burk, John Naglee. *Mozart and His Music.* New York: Random House, 1959.

Davenport, Marcia. *Mozart.* New York: Scribner & Sons, 1932.

Gheon, Henri. *In Search of Mozart.* New York: Sheed & Ward, Inc., 1934.

Holmes, Edward. *The Life of Mozart.* London: Chapman & Hall, 1845.

Hussey, Dyneley. *Wolfgang Amadeus Mozart.* Westport, CT: Greenwood Press, 1971.

King, Alexander Hyatt. *A Biography with a Survey of Books, Editions and Recordings.* London: Oxford University Press, 1970.

Kolb, Annette. *Mozart.* London: V. Gollancz, Ltd, 1939.

Langdon, Howard Chandler Robbins. *The Mozart Companion.* New York: Oxford University Press, 1956.

Levey, Michael. *The Life and Death of Mozart.* London: Weidenfeld and Nicolson, 1971.

Novello, Vincent. *A Mozart Pilgrimage.* London: Ernst Eulenburg, Ltd., 1975.

Robertson, Alec. *Requiem, Music of Mourning and Consolation.* New York: F. A. Praeger, 1968.

Sadie, Stanley. *Mozart.* London: Calder & Boyars, 1966.

Notes for Chapter 5 — Ludwig Van Beethoven

1   Michael Hamburger, *Beethoven, Letters, Journals, and Conversations* (Gordon City: Doubleday & Co., Inc. 1960), pp. 32.

2   Ibid., pp. 31-32.

3   Ates Orga, *Beethoven, His Life and Times* (Neptune City, New Jersey: Paganiniana Publications, 1980), p. 135.

4   Maynard Solomon, *Beethoven Essays* (Cambridge: Harvard University Press, 1988),. p. 218.

5   Robert W. S. Mendl, *The Divine Quest in Music* (New York: Philosophical Library, 1957), p. 86.

6   Ibid., pp. 86-87.

7   Howard Chandler Robbins Langdon, *Beethoven: A Documentary Study* (New York: MacMillan Publishing Co., 1970), pp. 205-206.

8   Elliott Forbes, *Thayer's Life of Beethoven* (Princeton: Princeton University Press, 1973), p. 482.

9   Anton Felix Schindler, *Beethoven as I Knew Him* (London: Faber & Faber, 1966), p. 365.

10 James Burnett, *Beethoven and Human Destiny* (New York: Roy Publishing, 1966), p. 19.

11 Solomon, op. cit., p. 216.

12 Ibid, pp. 216-217.

13 Friedrich Kerst, *Beethoven, the Man and the Artist, as Revealed in His Own Words* (New York: Dover, 1964), p. 104.

14 Solomon, op. cit., p. 223.

15 Ibid., p. 223.

16 Mendl, op. cit., p. 87.

17 Kerst, op. cit., p. 106.

18 Philip Kruseman, *Beethoven's Own Words* (London: Hinricksen Edition, 1947), p. 53.

19 Ibid, p. 53.

20 George R. Marek, *Beethoven, Biography of a Genius* (London: William Kimber, 1969), p. 177.

21 Mendl, op. cit., p. 86.

22 Marek, op. cit., p. 177.

23 Solomon, op. cit., pp. 220-221.

24 Ibid., p. 228.

25 Hugh Reginald Haweis, *Music and Morals,* (New York: Harper & Brothers, 1900), pp. 85-86.

26 Alan Tyson, "The 1803 Version of Beethoven's Christus am Oelberge", The Musical Quarterly, Vol. LVI, No. 4 (October 1970), p. 551.

27 Solomon, op. cit., p. 220.

28 Ibid., pp. 218-219.

29   Joseph De Marliave, *Beethoven's Quartets* (New York: Dover Publications, 1961), p. 328.

30   Paul Miles, *Beethoven's Sketches* (New York: Dover Publications, 1974), p. 154.

31   Warren Kirkendale, "New Roads to Old Ideas in Beethoven's Missa Solemnis", The Musical Quarterly, Vol. LVI, No. 4 (October 1970), p. 676.

32   George Grove, *Beethoven and His Nine Symphonies* (New York: Dover Publications, 1962), p. 326.

33   Marek, op. cit., p. 179.

34   Mendl, op. cit., p. 91.

35   J. W. N. Sullivan, *Beethoven, His Spiritual Development* (New York: Mentor Books, 1927), p. 118.

36   Mendl, op. cit., p. 93

37   Wilfred Mellers, *Beethoven and the Voice of God* (New York: Oxford University Press, 1983), p. 3.

38   Marek, op. cit., p. 560.

39   John N. Burk, *The Life and Works of Beethoven* (New York: Random House, Inc., 1943), p. 206.

40   Marek, op. cit., p. 561.

41   Irving Kolodin, *The Interior Beethoven* (New York: Alfred A. Knopf, 1975), p. 268.

OTHER SOURCES:

Anderson, Emily. *The Letters of Beethoven.* London: St. Martin's Press, 1961.

Anderson, Emily. "The Text of Beethoven's Letters". Music and Letters, xxxiv, 1953, p. 192.

Arnold, Denis and Fortune, Nigel, Editors. *The Beethoven Companion.* London: Faber, 1971.

Crowest, Frederick James. *Beethoven.* London: J. M. Dent & Company, 1904.

Grace, Harvey. *Ludwig van Beethoven.* London: K. Paul, Trench, Trubner, & Company, Ltd., 1927.

Howes, Frank Stewart. *Beethoven.* London: Oxford University Press, 1933.

Lang, Paul Henry, editor. *The Creative World of Beethoven.* New York: W. W. Norton & Company, 1971.

Newman, Ernest. *The Unconscious Beethoven.* New York: A. A. Knopt, 1970.

Rolland, Romain. *Beethoven the Creator.* New York: Dover Publications, 1964.

Sadie, Stanley. *Beethoven.* New York: Crowell Company, 1967.

Schmidt-Gorg, Joseph. *Ludwig van Beethoven.* New York: Praeger, 1970.

Specht, Richard. *Beethoven as He Lived.* London: Macmillan & Company, Ltd., 1933.

Solomon, Maynard. "Beethoven: The Nobility Pretense". Musical Quarterly, lxi, 1975, p. 272.

Sonneck, Oscar George. *Beethoven Letters in America.* New York: G. Schirmer, Inc., 1927.

NOTES FOR CHAPTER 6 - FRANZ PETER SCHUBERT

1   Otto Erich Deutsch, *Schubert, Memoirs of His Friends* (London: Adam & Charles Black, LTD, 1958), pp. 184-185.

2   George Lowell Austin, *The Life of Franz Schubert* (Boston: Shepard & Gill, 1873, p. 10.

3   Deutsch, op. cit., p. 52.

4   Otto Erich Deutsch, *Schubert: A Documentary Biography* (New York: Da Capo Press, 1977), pp. 822-823.

5   Maurice J. E. Brown, *Schubert, A Critical Biography* (New York: St. Martin's Press, 1958), p. 13.

6   Robert Haven Schauffler, *Franz Schubert, the Ariel of Music* (New York: G. P. Putnam's Sons, 1949), p. 27.

7   Deutsch, *Schubert, Memoirs of His Friends,* op. cit., p. 57.

8   Ibid., p. 184.

9   Heinrich Kreissle Von Hellborn, *The Life of Franz Schubert,* Vol. I, (New York: Vienna House, 1972), p. 12.

10 Deutsch, Schubert: *A Documentary Biography,* op. cit., p. 571.

11 Ibid., p. 572.

12 Newman Flower, *Franz Schubert* (London: Cassell & Company, Ltd., 1928), p. 24.

13 Otto Erich Deutsch, editor, *Franz Schubert's Letters and Other Writings* (London: Faber & Gwyer, LTD, 1928), p. 29.

14 Karl Kobald, *Franz Schubert and His Times* (London: Kennikat Press, 1928), p. 112.

15 Ralph Bates, *Franz Schubert* (Edinburgh: Peter Davies, LTD, 1934), p. 76.

16 Flower, op. cit., p. 53.

17 Alfred Einstein, *Schubert, A Musical Biography* (New York: Oxford University Press, 1951), pp. 312-313.

18 Peggy Woodford, *Schubert, His Life and Times* (Kent: Midas Books, 1978), p. 135.

19 Ibid., p. 134.

20 Carl A. Abram, from *The Music of Schubert*, edited by Gerald Abraham (New York: N. N. Norton & Company, 1947), pp. 225-226.

21 Oskar Bie, *Schubert, The Man* (Westport: Greenwood Press, 1971), p. 192.

22 Dietrich Fischer-Dieskau, *Schubert, A Biographical Study of His Songs* (London: Cassell & Company, LTD, 1971), p. 127.

23 John Reed, *Schubert, the Final Years* (London: Faber & Faber, LTD, 1972), p. 239.

24 Maurice J. E. Brown, *Essays on Schubert* (New York: St. Martin's Press, 1966), p. 124.

25 Reed, op. cit., p 219.

26 Austin, op. cit., pp. 51-52.

27 Reed, op. cit., p. 239.

28 Deutsch, *Schubert: A Documentary Biography*, op. cit., p. 598.

29 Reed, op. cit., p. 239.

OTHER SOURCES

Brown, Maurice John Edwin. *Schubert's Variations.* London: St. Martin's Press, 1954.

Capell, Richard. *Schubert's Songs.* London: E. Benn Ltd., 1928.

Clutsam, George H. *Schubert.* New York: F. A. Stokes & Company, 1912.

Cone, E. T. "Schubert's Beethoven". Musical Quarterly, lvi, 1970, p. 779.

Deutsch, Otto Erich. "The Riddle of Schubert's Unfinished Symphony". The Music Review, i, 1940, p. 36.

Deutsch, Otto Erich. *The Schubert Reader.* New York: W. W. Norton & Company, 1947.

Duncan, Edmond Stoune. *Schubert.* London: J. M. Dent & Company, 1905.

Paine, John Knowles. *The History of Music to the Death of Schubert.* London: Ginn & Company, 1907.

Schneider, Marcel. *Schubert.* New York: Grove Press, 1959.

NOTES FOR CHAPTER 7 - FELIX MENDELSSOHN

1 Ferdinand Hiller, *Mendelssohn, Letters and Recollections* (New York: Vienna House, l972), p. 84.

2 Eric Werner, *Mendelssohn: A New Image of the Composer and His Age* (London: Collier-MacMillan, Ltd., 1963), p. 38.

3 Ibid., p. 37.

4 Sebastian Hensel, *The Mendelssohn Family: From Letters and Journals* (VI) (Westport: Greenwood Press, 1968), p. 74.

5 Werner, op. cit., p. 37.

6 Ibid., p. 42.

7 George R. Marek, *Gentle Genius, the Story of Felix Mendelssohn* (New York: Funk & Wagnalls, 1972), p. 103.

8 Werner, op. cit., pp. 43-44.

9 Ibid., p. 208.

10 Schima Kaufman, *Mendelssohn, "A Second Elijah"* (Westport: Greenwood Press, l962), p. 87.

11 Herbert Kupferberg, *The Mendelssohns; Three Generations of Genius* (New York: Charles Scribner's Sons, 1972), p. 130.

12 Gerald Hendrie, *Mendelssohn's Rediscovery of Bach* (Buckinghamshire: The Open University Press, 1971), p. 27.

13 Kupferberg, op. cit., p. 146.

14 Edward Devrient, *My Recollections of Felix Mendelssohn-Bartholdy* (New York: Vienna House, 1972), p. 302.

15 Philip Radcliffe, *Mendelssohn* (London: J. M. Dent & Sons, Ltd., 1967), p. 36.

16 Marek, op. cit., p. 257.

17   Heinrich Edward Jacob, *Felix Mendelssohn and His Times* (Englewood Cliffs, New Jersey: Prentice-Hall, Inc., 1963), p. 220.

18   Elise Polko, *Reminiscences of Felix Mendelssohn-Bartholdy* (New York: Leypoldt & Holt, 1869), p. 115-116.

19   Frederick George Edwards, *The History of Mendelssohn's Oratorio "Elijah"* (London: Novello, Ewer & Co., 1896), p. 13.

20   W. F. Alexander, editor, *Selected Letters of Mendelssohn* (London: Swan Sonnenschein & Co., 1894), P. 96.

21   Werner, op. cit., p. 42.

22   Hensel, op. cit., p. 337.

23   Paul Mendelssohn, *Letters of Felix Mendelssohn-Bartholdy from 1833 to 1847* (Freeport, New York: Books for Libraries Press, 1970), p. 383.

24   Hiller, op. cit., p. 85.

25   Jacob, op. cit., p. 216.

26   Werner, op. cit., p. 283.

27   Jacob, op. cit., p. 216.

28   Ibid., p. 91.

29   Mendelssohn, op. cit., p. 63.

30   Ibid., p. 147.

31   Kaufman, op. cit., p. 304.

OTHER SOURCES:

Adolf, Wilheim. *Life of Felix Mendelssohn Bartholdy.* Boston: O. Ditson & Company, 1866.

Bennett, R. Sterndale. "The Death of Mendelssohn". Musical Quarterly, xxxvi, 1955, p. 374.

Blunt, Wilfrid. *On Wings of Song: A Biography of Felix Mendelssohn.* London: Hamish Hamilton Ltd., 1974.

Hurd, Michael. *Mendelssohn.* New York: T. Y Crowell Company, 1971.

Jenkins, David. *Mendelssohn in Scotland.* New York: Chappell, 1978.

Mendelssohn-Bartholdy, Felix, Seldon-Goth, G., editor. *Felix Mendelssohn's Letters.* New York: Vienna House, 1973.

Mendelssohn, Karl. *Mendelssohn and Goethe.* London: Macmillan & Company, 1872.

Moscheles, Felix. *Fragments of an Autobiography.* London: J. Nisbet & Company, Ltd., 1899.

Petitpierre, Jacque. *The Romance of the Mendelssohns.* London: D. Dobson, 1947.

Stratton, Stephen Samuel. *Mendelssohn.* London: J. M. Dent & Sons, Ltd., 1934.

Binck, Thomas Lindsay. *Elijah, The Story of Mendelssohn's Oratorio.* New Plymouth: Thomas Avery & Sons, Ltd., 1935.

NOTES FOR CHAPTER 8 - FRANZ LISZT

1   Louis Nohl, *The Life of Liszt* (Chicago: Jansen, McClurg, & Company, 1884), p. 128.

2   Ann M. Lingg, *Mephisto Waltz: The Story of Franz Liszt* (New York; Henry Holt & Company, 1951), p. 11.

3   Ernest Newman, *The Man Liszt* (New York: Taplinger Publishing Company, 1935), pp. 29-30.

4   Raphael Ledos de Beaufort, *The Abbe Liszt, The Story of His Life* (London: Ward & Downey, 1886), p. 101.

5   Newman, op. cit., p. 30.

6   T. Carlaw Martin, *Franz Liszt* (London: William Reeves, 1886), p. 13.

7   Anthony Wilkinson, *Liszt* (London: MacMillan London LTD, 1975), p. 37.

8   Sacheverell Sitwell, *Liszt* (London: Cassell & Company, LTD, 1955), p. 144.

9   William Wallace, *Liszt, Wagner, and the Princess* (New York: E. P. Dutton & Company, 1927), p. 102.

10   Sitwell, op. cit., pp. 238-239.

11   Claude Rostrand, *Liszt* (London: Calder & Boyars, 1972), p. 150.

12   Eleanor Perenzi, *Liszt* (London: Weidenfeld & Nicolson, 1974), p. 108.

13   Ibid, p. 108.

14   Paul Roes, *Music, the Mystery and the Reality* (Chevy Chase, Maryland: E. & M. Publishing, 1955), p. 7.

15 Lina Ramann, *Franz Liszt, Artist and Man* (London: W.H. Allen & Company, 1882), p. 384.

16 Lingg, op. cit., p. 221.

17 Rostrand, op. cit., p. 151.

18 Bence Szabolcsi, *The Twilight of Liszt* (Boston: Crescendo Publishing Company, 1956), pp., 65-66.

19 Rostrand, op. cit., p. 156-157.

20 De Beaufort, op. cit, p. 195.

21 Lingg, op. cit., p. 259.

22 Perenzi, op. cit., p. 104.

23 Ramann, op. cit., p. 373.

24 Franz Liszt, *Letters of Franz Liszt,* edited by La Mara. (New York: Greenwood Press, 1969), p. 14.

25 Hugh Reginald Hawais, *My Musical Memories* (New York: Funk & Wagnalls, 1884), p. 267.

26 Franz Liszt, *Correspondence of Wagner and Liszt,* translated by Francis Hueffer. (New York: Vienna House, 1973), p. 273.

27 Franz Liszt, *The Letters of Franz Liszt to Marie zu Sayn-Wittgenstein,* edited by Howard E. Hugo. (Westport, CT: Greenwood Press 1971), p. 128.

28 Ibid., p. 234.

29 Ibid., p. 144.

30 Ibid., p. 83.

31 James Huneker, *Franz Liszt* (New York: Charles Scribner's Sons, 1924), p. 98.

32 Sitwell, op. cit., p. 224.

33 Wilkinson, op. cit., p. 38.

34 Sitwell, op. cit., p. 241.

35 Janka Wohl, *Liszt: Recollections of a Compatriot* (London: Ward & Downey, 1887), pp. 162-164.

36 Perenzi, Liszt, op. cit., p. 98.

37 Wilkinson, op. cit., p. 41.

38 Ibid., p. 41.

39 Ibid., p. 41.

OTHER SOURCES:

Auer, Leopold. *My Long Life in Music.* London, 1924.

Beckett, Walter. *Liszt.* London: J. M Dent, 1956.

Buchner, Alexandr. *Franz Liszt and His Music.* New York: John Lane Company, 1911.

Fay, Amy. *Music Study in Germany.* London: MacMillan & Co., 1886.

Habets, A., editor. *Letters of Liszt and Borodin.* London, 1895.

Hill, Ralph. *Liszt.* London: Duckworth, 1936.

Seroff, Victor. *Franz Liszt.* Freeport, New York: Books For Libraries Press, 1970.

Siloti, Alexander. *My Memories of Liszt.* Edinburgh: Methven Simpson, Ltd., 1911.

Strelezki, Anton. *Personal recollections of chats with Liszt.* London: E. Dunajowski & Co., 1893.

Von Lenz, William. *The Great Piano Virtuosos of Our Time.* New York: Regency Press, 1971.

NOTES FOR CHAPTER 9 - RICHARD WAGNER

1 Stewart Robb, foreword to his translation of *Wagner's Ring of the Nibelung* (New York: E. P. Dutton & Co., Inc., 1960), p. xxxiv.

2 Ibid., p. xxvi.

3 Peter Burdidge and Richard Sutton, *The Wagner Companion* (New York: Cambridge University Press, 1979), pp. 158 & 159.

4 Richard Wagner, *My Life* (New York: Dodd, Mead & Co., 1911), p. 23.

5 Ibid., p. 23.

6 Frederick Taber Cooper, *Richard Wagner* (New York: Frederick Stokes Co., 1915), p. 188.

7 George Bird, translator, *Diary of Richard Wagner,* 1865-82 (Cambridge University Press, 1980), p. 154.

8 Wagner, op. cit., p. 469.

9   Ibid., p. 469.
10 Hugh Frederick Garten, *Wagner the Dramatist* (Totowa, NJ: Rowman & Littlefield, 1977), pp. 65-66.
11 Richard Wagner, *Jesus of Nazareth* (Translated by William Ashton Ellis) (St. Clair Shores, Michigan: Scholarly Press, Inc., 1972), pp. 284-340.
12 Paul Bekker, *Richard Wagner, His Life in His Work* (Westport, CT: Greenwood Press, 1931), p. 478.
13 Wilhelm Altmann editor, *Letters of Richard Wagner* (London: D. M. Dent & Sons, 1936), p. 102.
14 Robb, op. cit., p. xxxii.
15 Ernest Newman, *Wagner, as Man and Artist* (New York: Tudor Publishing Co., 1924), p. 273.
16 John Chancellos, *Wagner* (Boston: Little, Brown & Co., 1978), pp. 264-265.
17 Ibid., p. 264.
18 Ibid., p. 265.
19 Robb, op. cit., p. xxxv
20 Ibid., p. xxxv.
21 Derek Watson, *Richard Wagner, A Biography* (London: J.M. Dent & Sons LTD, 1979), p. 304.
22 Robb, op. cit., p. xxxviii
23 Bird, op. cit., p. 202.
24 Robb, op. cit., p. xxxviii.
25 Ibid., p. xxxviii.
26 Ibid., p. xxxiv.
27 Watson, op. cit., p. 304.
28 Ibid., p. 304.
29 Robb, op. cit., p. xxxiv.
30 Watson, op. cit., p. 301.
31 Ibid., p. 303.
32 H. T. Finck, *Wagner and His Works; the Story of His Life* (New York: Greenwood Press, 1968), pp. 326-337.
33 Watson, op. cit., p. 302.
34 Robb, op. cit., p. xxvi.
35 Ibid., p. xxxii.
36 Watson, op. cit., pp. 305-306.
37 Chancellos, op. cit., p. 272.
38 Richard Wagner, "Religion and Art" (Translated by William Ashton Ellis) (St. Clair Shores, Michigan, 1972), p. 233.
39 Watson, op. cit., p. 302.
40 Ibid., p. 302.
41 Wagner, "Religion and Art", op. cit., p. 231.

OTHER SOURCES:

Abraham, G. "Nietzsche's Attitude to Wagner: A Fresh View". Music and Letters, xiii, 1932, p.64.
Aldrich, Richard. *A Guide to the Ring of the Nibelung.* New York: C. H. Ditson & Company, 1905.
Bennett, Joseph. *Letters from Bayreuth.* London: Novello, Ewer, 1877.
Burrell, Mary. *Richard Wagner: His Life and Works from 1813-1834.* London: 1898.
Chamberlain, Houston Stewart. *Richard Wagner.* Munich: F. Bruchmann, 1897.
Culshaw, John. *Ring Resounding.* New York: Viking Press, 1967.
Dannreuther, Edward. *Wagner and the Reform of Opera.* London: Augener & Company, 1904.
Deathridge, John. *Wagner's Rienzi.* New York: Clarendan Press, 1977.
Gal, Hans. *Richard Wagner.* London: Victor Gollancz Ltd., 1976.
Hueffer, Francis F. *Richard Wagner.* London: Chapman & Hall, Ltd., 1912.
Kufferath, Maurice. *The Parsifal of Richard Wagner.* New York: United States Book Company, 1892.
Von Westernhagen, Curt. *Wagner.* Zurich: Atlantis-Musik Buch-Verlag, 1979.
Wilson, Pearl Cleveland. *Wagner's Dramas and Greek Tragedy.* New York: Columbia University Press, 1919.

NOTES FOR CHAPTER 10 - ANTONIN DVORAK

1 Neil Butterworth, *Dvorak, His Life and Times* (Kent: Midas Books, 1980), p. 15.
2 Claire Lee Purdy, *Antonin Dvorak, Composer from Bohemia* (New York: Julian Messner, Inc., 1950), p. 112.
3 Otakar Sourek, *Antonin Dvorak, Letters and Reminiscences* (Prague: Artia Books, 1954), pp. 28-29.
4 Karel Hoffmeister, *Antonin Dvorak*, (Westport, CT: Greenwood Press, 1970), pp. 104-105.
5 Sourek, op. cit., p. 111.
6 Mosco Carner, "The Church Music", from *Antonin Dvorak, His Achievement*, Editor, Viktol Fischl, (Westport: Greenwood Press, 1970), pp. 167-168.
7 Sourek, op. cit., p. 111.
8 Paul Stefan, *Anton Dvorak* (New York: Da Capo Press, 1971), p. 291.
9 Sourek, op. cit., p. 112.
10 Ibid., p. 179.
11 Ibid., p. 213.
12 Gervase Hughes, *Dvorak, His Life and Music* (London: Cassell & Co., Ltd., 1967), p. 171.
13 Sourek, op. cit., pp. 192-193.
14 Butterworth, op. cit., p. 45.
15 Carner, op. cit., p. 169.
16 Jarmil Burchauser, *Antonin Dvorak* (Prague: Statni Hudebni Vydavatelstvi, 1967), p.6.
17 Hughes, op. cit., p. 128.
18 Otakar Sourek, *Antonin Dvorak, The Complete Edition* (Prague: Artio Books, 1956), p.44.
19 Vaclav Holzknect, *Antonin Dvorak*, (Prague: Orbis Books, 1971), pp. 64-65.
20 Carner, op. cit., p. 169.
21 Holzknect, op. cit., p. 66.
22 Carner, op. cit., pp. 166-167.
23 John Chapham, *Dvorak* (London: David & Charles, 1979), p. 163.
24 Sourek, *Antonin Dvorak, Letters and Reminiscences*, op. cit., p. 195.
25 Stefan, *Anton Dvorak*, op. cit., p. 291.
26 Ibid., p. 263.
27 Sourek, *Antonin Dvorak, Letters and Reminiscences*, op. cit., p. 112.
28 Ibid., pp. 111-112.
29 Olga Humlova, *Antonin Dvorak* (Prague: Orbis Books, 1954), p. 25.
30 Otakar Sourek, *Antonin Dvorak, Letters and Reminiscences*, op. cit., p. 28.

OTHER SOURCES:

Anonymous. "How Dr. Dvorak Gives a Lesson". New York Herald, January 14, 1894, p. 5.
Bennett, J. "The Music of Anton Dvorak". Music and Letters, xxii, 1881, pp. 165 & 236.
Chapham, John. "Dvorak and the American Indian". The Musical Times, cvii, 1966, p. 863.
Chapham, John. "Dvorak's Relations with Brahms and Hanslick". Musical Quarterly, lvii, 1971, p. 241.
Dagan, Avigdor. *Anton Dvorak: His Achievement*. Westport, CT: Greenwood Press, 1970.
Dvorak, Antonin. "Antonin Dvorak on Negro Melodies". New York Herald, May 25, 1893.
Fles, Barthold. *Slavonic Rhapsody*. New York: Allen, Towne, & Heath, 1948.
Kinscella, H. G. "Dvorak and Spillville: Forty Years After". Musical America, liii, May 25, 1933, p. 4.
Mason, Daniel Gregory. *From Grieg to Brahms*. New York: Macmillan Company, 1927.
Sourek, Otakar. *Anton Dvorak, His Life and Times*. New York: Philosophical Library, 1954.

NOTES FOR CHAPTER 11 - CHARLES IVES

1 John Kirkpatrick, "Charles Ives", in Grove's Dictionary of Music and Musicians, 5th edition, Eric Blom, editor (New York: St. Martin's Press. 1970), p. 503.
2 Vivian Perlis, editor, *Charles Ives Remembered: An Oral History* (New York: W. W. Norton & Co., 1974), pp. 76-77, and 114.

3   Ibid., p. 112.
4   Kirkpatrick, op. cit., p. 503.
5   Henry and Sidney Cowell, *Charles Ives and his Music* (New York: Da Capo Press, 1983), p. 30.
6   Kirkpatrick, op. cit., p. 508.
7   Ibid., p. 505.
8   Ibid., p. 505.
9   Ibid., p. 505.
10 John Kirkpatrick, editor, *Ives: Memos* (New York: W. W. Norton & Co., 1972), p. 128.
11 Wendell Clarke Kumlien, "The Sacred Choral Music of Charles Ives" (a dissertation for the University of
    Illinois, Urbana; Ann Arbor: Microfilms International, 1969), p. 39.
12 Rosalie Sandra Perry, *Charles Ives and the American Mind* (Kent, OH: Kent State University Press, 1974),
    p. 79.
13 Kumlien, op. cit., p. 40.
14 Perry, op. cit., pp. 77-80.
15 Kirkpatrick, "Charles Ives", op. cit., pp. 509-513.
16 Perry, op. cit., p. 75.
17 Frank R. Rossiter, *Charles Ives and His America* (New York: Liveright Publishers, 1975), p. 40.
18 Kirkpatrick, *Ives: Memos*, op. cit., p. 133.
19 Cowell, op. cit., p. 23.
20 Rossiter, op. cit., p. 39.
21 David Woolbridge, *From the Steeples and Mountains; A Study of Charles Ives* (New York: Alfred A. Knopf),
    p. 43.
22 Kirkpatrick, *Ives: Memos*, op. cit., p. 133.
23 Perry, op. cit., p. 89.
24 Perlis, op. cit., pp. 218.
25 James Peter Burkholder, *Charles Ives, The Man Behind the Ideas* (New Haven: Yale University Press, 1985),
    p. 104.
26 Perlis, op. cit., p. 77.
27 Ibid., p. 109.
28 Kirkpatrick, *Ives: Memos*, op. cit., p. 129.
29 Perlis, op. cit., p. 112.
30 Ibid., pp. 83 and 114.
31 Ibid., p. 77.
32 H. Wiley Hitchcock & Vivian Perlis, editors, *An Ives Collection* (Urbana: University of Illinois Press, 1977),
    p. 8-9.
33 Charles Ives, *Essays Before a Sonata* (New York, Dover Publications, 1945), p. 117.
34 Perlis, op. cit., p. 219.

OTHER SOURCES:

Ballantine, C. "Charles Ives and the Meaning of Quotation in Music". Musical Quarterly, lxv, 1979, p. 167.
Bellamann, H. "Charles Ives: The Man and His Music". Musical Quarterly, xix, 1933, p. 45.
Bellamann, H. "The Music of Charles Ives". Pro Musica, v/1, 1927.
Chase, G. "Composer from Connecticut". America's Music, New York, 1955, p. 653.
Copland, Aaron. "The Ives Case". Our New Music, New York, 1941, p. 149.
DeLerma, Dominique-Rene. *Charles E. Ives*. Kent, OH: Kent State University Press, 1970.
Elkus, Jonathan. *Charles Ives and the American Band Tradition*. University of Exeter: American Arts Docu-
    mentation Center, 1974.
Ives, Charles Edward. *Epilogue, with an Addendum*. New Haven CT: P. Boatright, 1956.
Marshall, D. "Charles Ives Quotations". Perspectives of New Music, vi, 1968, p. 45.
Moor, P. "On Horseback to Heaven". Harper's. cxcvii, 1948.
Sive, Helen R. *Music's Connecticut Yankee*. New York: Atheneum, 1977.
Sterne, C. "Quotation in Charles Ives' 2nd Symphony". Music and Letters, lii, 1971, p. 39.

Notes for Chapter 12 - Igor Stravinsky

1 Igor Stravinsky and Robert Craft, *Expositions and Developments* (Garden City: Doubleday & Co., Inc., 1962), pp. 61-63.

2 Eric Walter White, *Stravinsky, the Composer and His Work* (Berkeley: University of California Press, 1966), pp. 89-90.

3 Stravinsky and Craft, op. cit., p. 61.

4 Ibid., p. 63.

5 Ibid., p. 64.

6 White, op. cit., pp. 89-90.

7 Igor Stravinsky and Robert Craft, *Dialogues and a Diary* (Garden City: Doubleday & Co., Inc., 1962), p. 9. (Used by permission).

8 Vera Stravinsky and Robert Craft, *Stravinsky in Pictures and Documents*, (New York: Simon & Schuster, 1978), p. 295.

9 Roman Vlad, *Stravinsky* (New York: Oxford University Press, 1978), p. 157.

10 Stravinsky and Craft, *Dialogues and a Diary*, op. cit., pp. 77-78.

11 Francis Routh, *Stravinsky* (London: J.M. Dent & Sons, LTD, 1975), p. 119.

12 Alexandre Tansman, *Igor Stravinsky, The Man and His Music* (New York: G.P. Putnam's Sons, 1949), p. 129.

13 Gilbert Amy, "Aspects of the Religious Music of Igor Stravinsky," from *Confronting Stravinsky*, edited by Jann Pasler (Berkeley: University of California Press, 1986), p. 197.

14 Igor Stravinsky and Robert Craft, *Conversations with Igor Stravinsky* (Berkeley: University of California Press, 1958), p. 124.

15 Ibid., p. 125.

16 Igor Stravinsky and Robert Craft, *Themes and Episodes* (New York: Alfred A. Knopf, 1966), p. 350.

17 Stravinsky and Craft, *Expositions and Developments*, op. cit., p. 65.

18 Neil Tierney, *The Unknown Country (Life of Igor Stravinsky)* (London: Robert Hale Limited, 1977), p. 165.

19 Vlad, op. cit., p. 156.

20 Stravinsky and Craft, *Themes and Episodes*, op. cit., p. 31.

21 Vlad, op. cit., p. 164.

22 Stravinsky and Craft, *Dialogues and a Diary*, op. cit., p. 90.

23 Ibid., p. 96.

24 Ibid., p. 97.

25 Ibid, p. 25.

26 Ibid, p. 23.

27 Ibid, p. 79.

28 Robert Craft, "1949, Stravinsky's Mass, A Notebook", from *Igor Stravinsky*, edited by Edwin Cole (New York: Duell, Sloan, & Pearce, 1949), p. 206.

29 Igor Stravinsky, *Poetics of Music* (Cambridge: Harvard University Press, 1947), p. 142.

Other Sources:

Armitage, Merle, editor. *Igor Stravinsky*. New York: G. Schirmer, Inc., 1936.

Boretz, Benjamin and Cone, Edward, editors. *Perspectives on Schoenberg and Stravinsky*. New York: W. W. Norton & Co., 1972.

Corle, Edwin E., editor. *Igor Stravinsky*. New York: Duell, Sloan, & Pearce, 1949.

Craft, Robert. *Bravo Stravinsky*. New York: World Publishing Co., 1967.

Craft, Robert. *Stravinsky, Chronicle of a Friendship*. New York: A. A. Knopf, 1972.

Horgan, Paul. *Encounters with Stravinsky: A Personal Record*. New York: Farrar, Staus, & Giroux, 1972.

Lang, Paul Henry. *Stravinsky, A New Appraisal of His Work*. New York: W. W. Norton & Co., 1963.

Lederman, Minna. *Stravinsky in the Theatre*. New York: Da Capo Press, 1975.

Libman, Lillian. *And Music at the Close: Stravinsky's Last Years, A Personal Memoir*. New York: W. W. Norton & Co., 1972.

McCauldin, Denis. *Stravinsky*. London: Novello, 1972.

Myers, Rollo. *Introduction to the Music of Stravinsky.* London: Dobson, 1950.

Stravinsky, Igor and Craft, Robert. *Memories and Commentaries.* Berkley: University of California Press, 1960.

Stravinsky, Igor and Craft, Robert. *Retrospectives and Conclusions.* New York: A. A. Knopf, 1969.

White, Eric Walter. *Stravinsky: A Critical Study.* New York: Philosophical Library, 1948.

About the author -

Patrick Kavanaugh

Patrick Kavanaugh is well known as a composer, conductor, lecturer, and as the Executive Director of the Christian Performing Artists' Fellowship. As the conductor of the Asaph Ensemble, he has performed at the Kennedy Center Concert Hall and Terrace Theatre, the Lisner Auditorium, Constitution Hall, Folger Theatre, the National Presbyterian Center, Gaston Hall, and Alden Theatre. Author of the book, *The Spiritual Lives of Great Composers,* he has lectured extensively on this subject, at universities, churches, the National Portrait Gallery, and the State Department.

Born in Nashville, Tennessee in 1954, Kavanaugh's musical education includes a Bachelor of Music from the CUA School of Music, a Master of Music and a Doctor of Musical Arts, both from the University of Maryland, where he served for three years as a Graduate Fellow. He has also done extensive Post-Doctoral work in musicology, music theory, and conducting. His teachers have included Conrad Bernier, Mark Wilson, George Thaddeus Jones, and Lloyd Geisler.

As a composer, he currently has eighteen compositions published by Carl Fischer, Inc., licensed by Broadcast Music, Inc. (BMI). Kavanaugh has composed in a wide variety of genre, from orchestral to chamber music, from opera to electronic music. Larger works include his opera *The Last Supper,* a ballet *The Song of Songs,* and orchestral pieces *Jack in the Beanstalk* (for 148 musicians, all on separate parts), *Three Poems of George Herbert,* and *Prelude to the Last Letter of John Keats.* His many chamber compositions include fourteen solo pieces (the *Debussy Variations* series), five quartets, the *New Testament Suite, The Art of the Maze,* and the *Homage to C.S. Lewis.* His many performances include such unusual works as the *Symphonic Parade* (premiered in the middle of Wisconsin Avenue in Georgetown), *Jubal* (for "self-accompanied" soprano), and *Music of the Spheres,* which received extensive national attention in 1975.

The favorable response to his work has been remarkable. "Dr. Patrick Kavanaugh offered a spectacular performance," claims the *Courier,* and the *Uptown Citizen* called him, "a gifted man, whose love and joy in his work are evident." The *Washington Post* notes that "His goal in creating this unusual concept is to take contemporary (classical) music out of just the conservatory and get it out to a large scale public," while *Accent Magazine* praises Kavanaugh's music as, "an attempt to meet the musical public on its own ground." One astonished editor declared that, "Attempting to explain Patrick Kavanaugh's compositions is comparable to delivering a precise and simplified explanation of nuclear theory." The *Journal Newpapers* commented, "A bust of Kavanaugh? Well, not quite yet, but judging from the young composer's progress, the first early motions have already been chipped into expression."

Dr. Kavanaugh now serves in full-time capacity as the Executive Director of the Christian Performing Artists' Fellowship. He resides in Vienna, Virginia, with his wife, Barbara, and their four children.

The Christian Performing Artists' Fellowship

The Christian Performing Artists' Fellowship (CPAF) is a classical music and dance ministry dedicated to performing classical music to the glory of God and to spreading the Gospel of Jesus Christ. Begun in 1984, it has attracted over 500 Christian musicians and dancers to its ranks.

Dr. Richard Halverson, Chaplain to the United States Senate, wrote after a recent CPAF performance, "It was outstanding. The orchestra, chorus and soloists - all believers - were of the highest professional calibre. The dance troupe and choreography were inspiring, exalting the Lord and his glory." *Christianity Today* notes that CPAF, "strives to bring the Gospel to a relatively overlooked group: the secular arts world." The *National Christian Reporter* calls CPAF members "missionaries", who are "all dedicated to bring the Gospel of Christ to those who might otherwise not hear it."

As a totally unique Christian ministry, CPAF members have performed for thousands in some of the most noted halls in the Washington, D.C. area including the Kennedy Center Concert Hall, the Lisner Auditorium, Constitution Hall, Alden Theatre, Gaston Hall, and the National Portrait Gallery. CPAF performers - instrumentalists, singers, and dancers - come from over 200 churches and some 25 different denominations.

CPAF has performed and choreographed such major works as Mozart's *Requiem*, the Bach *Magnificat* and *B Minor Mass*, Stravinsky's *Symphony of Psalms*, the Brahms *Requiem*, and in 1989 the premiere of a acclaimed annual event in Washington: CPAF's choreographed version of Handel's *Messiah*. In 1991, CPAF presented its first opera production at the Kennedy Center, featuring Metropolitan Opera star Jerome Hines in the title role of Boito's *Mefistofele*. Many CPAF performing groups called Selah Ensembles (String Quartet, Woodwind Quintet, Brass Quintet, Dance Troupe, etc.) now perform throughout the Washington, D.C. area, and chapters are being established in other cities. The largest CPAF group, the ASAPH ENSEMBLE (named after King David's chief musician), consists of combining a large orchestra, chorus, and dance company.

All CPAF performances are free of charge, so that no one is hindered from hearing the performance or their message for lack of funds. All expenses, including hall rentals, printing, publicity, and mailing, are met by donations, given by individuals who appreciate CPAF's unique ministry. The Christian Performing Artists' Fellowship is a registered non-profit, tax-exempt organization. For more information on CPAF call (703) 385-CPAF.

The Christian Performing Artists' Fellowship
10523 Main Street - Suite 31, Fairfax, Virginia 22030

Acknowledgements

This book represents the work and support of more people than I could possibly hope to thank, but I cannot forgo mentioning the following:

- The Directors of the Christian Performing Artists' Fellowship, Jim and Mary Jeane Kraft, Bob and Robin Sturm, Dennis and Jan Patrick, for their continued encouragement through the years of research, program notes, performances, and lectures.

- Jan Patrick, Wanda Skinner, Marthellen Hoffman, Connie Boltz, and Melanie Jeschke, for their excellent secretarial and artistic skills in preparing the manuscript.

- The distinguished staff of the Library of Congress in Washington, D.C., for their assistance with original manuscripts, photographs, and research of the text.

- David Hazard and Beth Spring, for their invaluable help in editing the book.

- Bill Hearn, and Billy Ray Hearn of the Sparrow Corporation, for their enthusiastic support and commitment to excellence.

- For the inspiration of my father, Edward J. Kavanaugh, the "other author" of the family.

- I especially want to express gratitude to my wife, Barbara, and my wonderful children, Christopher, John, Peter and David, for their infinite patience with a Dad who stays up long into the night reading and typing.